THOMAS COOK

Evangelist
and Saint

l+m4

Herbert Boyd McGonigle

MA, BD, DD, PHD

Former Lecturer at Nazarene Theological College, Dene Road, Didsbury, Manchester, in the classes in Church History, Theology and Wesley Studies, Former Principal of Nazarene Theological College and now Principal Emeritus

British Library Cataloguing in Publication Data.
A catalogue record for this book is available from the British Library

ISBN 978 0 86071 708 9

A Commissioned Publication of

MOORLEYS
Print & Publishing
tel: 0115 932 0643 web: www.moorleys.co.uk

FOREWORD

It is with great favour and grace that I am allowed to print the Revd. Les Evans reading of this book. Jeanne and I knew Les and Anna for almost fifty years and it is with great pleasure that we print his introduction. After studying at Hurlet Nazarene College (later to become Nazarene Theological College, NTC), Les pastored churches at Brownflow Fold, Bolton, Edmonton in Alberta, Fenton and Sheffield. He came to Manchester as NTC as Chaplin, lecturer in Homiletics and Pastoral Theology and to serve as Pastor of the newly opened Didsbury Church. He served in Manchester for five years and took on the Oldham Church, Manchester, and after three years, he and Anna retired from the full-time pastorate. Les was a fine preacher and Jeanne and I would go to hear him explaining and expounding the Word. We shared together in many Churches of the Nazarene and were together in many Convention services. Les knows about Thomas Cook's evangelistic services and the Lord blessing him as he preached about the glorious blessing of perfect love. Please read what Les has said and then you will be blessed as you read his life.

I count it an honour and a privilege to be invited to write the foreword to Dr. McGonigle's latest book – *Thomas Cook, Evangelist and Saint*. Reading through the manuscript, we find all the characteristics we have come to expect from the author: painstaking research, effective organising of material and a relevant message for today's church.

In the reading of this work, one thing I can testify to without any exaggeration is, to quote John Wesley's famous words, 'I felt my heart strangely warmed.' There are two reasons for my enthusiastic response to this invitation to write the foreword, both of them very personal. I have known the author right from the beginning of his ministry in the Church of the Nazarene, covering both his pastoral work and as Principal of the Nazarene Theological College in Manchester. Over these fifty-five years I have valued the friendship forged, together with my deep appreciation of Dr. McGonigle's gifts in preaching, lecturing and writing.

The second reason for my enthusiasm is connected to the latest book itself. The first book I ever read on the theme of Christian Holiness, apart from the Bible itself, was Thomas Cook's *New Testament Holiness*, reviving memories of those early days. I was a teenager at the time, struggling to understand the distinctive of the Nazarene Church on this vital subject, and Cook's plain, lucid style was immensely valuable and enriched my life significantly.

As to Dr. McGonigle's book itself, this is no mere record of a preacher's life and work, it is a soul-stirring challenge of what God can still do through Spirit-filled men and women. A great deal of the book is taken up with the account of Cook's remarkable evangelistic ministry in many parts of the world, which, by any standards was quite amazing, for thousands of people were led into the Kingdom of God, and believers brought into a deeper walk with the Lord. What was the secret? There is a significant passage in this book which is worth quoting to give answer to this question. 'Very early in life Thomas first noticed in his reading that the great evangelists in Methodism had enjoyed a Pentecost in their lives and that this contributed largely to their increase of souls. He began to seek the second blessing which altered his life as much as the first blessing, and from Cook's experience of that blessing, there is shown his great usefulness of his ministry.'

We then have Cook's personal testimony of the difference this deeper work of grace made, not only in the recipient's heart, but in all his subsequent ministry of preaching and evangelism. Unhesitatingly, Cook pinpoints what brought this power in his preaching. Dr. McGonigle brings before us the preacher's words. 'Before we receive our Pentecost there is not much service worth the name. With the promised baptism the apostles entered upon a new phase of life and work. And so it is today. Christian life begins at Calvary, but effective service begins with the baptism of fire. Nobody ever was, or ever will be, saved, only through the preaching of the Gospel. It is the Gospel applied and enforced by the Holy Spirit that saves men.'

We are still slow to learn that basic New Testament truth. Here, then, is a message the contemporary church needs to both hear and embrace, and we are indebted to Dr. McGonigle for bringing to the church, through the life and work of Thomas Cook, a vital truth we desperately need in our day. I would venture to suggest that if this book is read with any kind of spiritual sensitivity, it will challenge afresh the nature of our walk with God and the quality and effectiveness of our service.

Revd. Leslie Evans
December 2015

THOMAS COOK
Evangelist and Saint

Speaking of the need to have, *Double Need and Double Cure*, Thomas Cook (1859-1912), shows that Dr. William Burt Pope (1822-1903), Manchester, spoke highly of a double great work of grace at a meeting for the deepening of spiritual life.

> I have sometimes very delicately scrupled at this, and, other expressions, and I have wondered if is right to speak of a 'second blessing;' and I have taken a text in which our Saviour takes a blind man and partially restores him his sight; and then, holding the man up before us for a little while, that we may study his state, which is a great advance upon what it was, that we may watch him in this state of struggle between sin and the flesh, He touches him again, and he sees every man clearly. In the face of that text, and in the face of the testimonies of multitudes now living, and in the face of the deep instinct, the hope and desire of my own unworthy heart, I will never again write against the phraseology referred to.[1]

Thomas Cook quotes this in defence of a 'second blessing', and he uses Dr. Burt Pope as an example of how scripture means a second definite work of grace.

Thomas Cook was born in Middlesbrough, Yorkshire, on July 20, 1859. Immediately after his birth his parents moved away from the town as his father was made foreman of some iron-works in the vicinity. The parents sent the two boys to an adjacent school and they attended the services of the Church of England. In course of time the family moved back to Middlesbrough and joined the congregation of the South Bank Wesleyan Methodist Chapel. Thomas was impressed with the preaching of Revd. James Nance on the subject of the voice of 'harpers with their harps' (Rev. 5:8) and it led to his conversion. He joined the Sunday School and was very impressed with his teacher who was a railway porter. In 1875, when he was sixteen years old,

---

[1] Thomas Cook, *New Testament Holiness*, (1902), p.31.

some special meetings for prayer were held in the circuit and Thomas was soundly converted as he stood before the communion rail.

Thomas immediately began to witness to his faith and he made a covenant that he would at least speak to one. Crossing the road one day, he saw a man pushing a hand-cart and he asked him whether he knew the Saviour of men and women. The man said he didn't know and invited Thomas to his house. He met them in their house and led the couple to the Lord and so it was that Thomas gathered his first sheaves. He was invited to join a Mission Band and saying, when he recounted his service, that he was ready to join the Salvation Army, but a pillar of cloud led him in another direction and greatly to the advancement of his own Church.

About this time William Morley Punshon (1824-1881), was visiting Middlesbrough and he appealed to young men to offer for the Christian ministry. Thomas Cook was there and he listened to Punshon's words and he felt himself to be part of the Lord's anointing. No fire fell on this occasion but for Thomas it was the chance to assure himself that this was God's will and he regarded himself as called to the ministry. He became a pupil teacher and he asked a local preacher to introduce his name to the Local Preacher's Meeting. The reply was that young men did not take the first step themselves but waited for Church to come to them. At the Christmas quarterly meeting in 1878, he was received as a fully credited local preacher after being examined in theology and kindred subjects. Thomas found great profit in reading John Wesley's *Journals*, John Fletcher's *Works*, William Arthur's *Tongue of Fire*, *Methodist Biography*, and Richard Watson's *Institutes*.

He received a letter from the Revd. J. H. Norton and the advice he received from it cannot be lost in discovering Cook's call.
> If you take a text, let it be a plain one. First, understand it yourself, then try to make those whom you address understand it.... Paul was inspired but he wanted the books and the parchments. Redeem your time. Rise early. Do not attempt too much. Never be unemployed but guard against busy idleness. Never forget that there is a time to be

silent, as well a time to speak. Connect all you do with God the Holy Ghost. He will help your infirmities. He will sanctify your nature, and comfort you under all your trials.[2]

From the first, God was pleased to use Thomas Cook in the conversion of sinners. During the two years that Thomas was a local preacher, even with his youthfulness and inexperience, his ministry was richly blessed of God. His services were not confined to his own Church but were freely given to the Primitive Methodists, the Salvation Army and other denominations. He preached and rejoiced over conversions and in that two years, three hundred people saw their names written in the Book of Life.

He held the first mission at Espland Hill, near Appleby and conversions took place. He visited Newcastle-on-Tyne where he ministered to large crowds. About this time Thomas had a dream and he thought he was standing by a lake that was crowded with fish and a voice said to him, 'I will make you a fisher of men.' (Mark 1:17).[3] Thomas Cook interpreted it as a statement and in the turn of events, his dream was correct. Very early in life Thomas first noticed in his reading that the great evangelists in Methodism had enjoyed a Pentecost in their lives and that this contributed largely to their increase of souls. He began to seek the second blessing which altered his life as much as the first blessing, and from Cook's experience of that blessing, there is shown his great usefulness of his ministry. From the small tract, entitled, *Thomas Cook's Experience*, there is found exactly what happened.

My conversation was so clear and satisfactory that I could never doubt its reality. The beginnings of this life of loyalty and love I shall never forget. It seems but as yesterday, though ten years have now passed since the love of God was shed abroad in my heart, and I was reconciled to God, who loved me, even me.... My highly-wrought emotions subsided, and petty annoyances of life chafed, the temptations of the devil assailed; and then I found out, as pride, envy, unbelief, self-will, and other forms of heart-sin stirred within me....The

---

[2] Henry Smart, *Thomas Cook's Early Ministry*, (1892), pp.29, 30.
[3] Henry Smart, *Thomas Cook's Early Ministry*, p.33.

'old man' was bound, but not cast out; the disease was modified, but not eradicated; sin was suspended, but its pollutions continued.... How many headaches and heartaches I had in struggling with my bosom foes no language can describe. All the while I was enjoying sweet fellowship with Christ, was blessedly conscious of acceptance in Him, was an earnest worker in the Lord's vineyard, and would rather have died than wilfully sinned against Him.... Reading Methodist biographies about this time stirred my heart, and filled me with hope for better things.... At this very juncture, when I felt I must die unless I received the grace, Mr. Joshua Dawson came into our town, and proclaimed full salvation to be a present duty and privilege.... I fell upon my knees, with the determination not to rise again until my request was granted.... If I walked in the light, the full cleansing from sin was my heritage. Without a moment's hesitation I did so, and cried out at the top of my voice, 'I claim the blessing now.' While they sang, the refining fire came down and went through my heart – searching, probing, melting, burning, filling all its chambers with light, and hallowing my heart to God.... Six beautiful years have passed away since then. But no words can ever express the complete satisfaction I have in Christ; the sweet sense of rest in His hallowing presence from all worry and care.... and the clear and indubitable witness of cleansing through the blood of Jesus.... How I wish I could tell of the sweetness, and richness, and indescribable blessedness of this life of perfect love.[4]

In 1880 he was nominated as a candidate for the Wesleyan ministry in the quarterly meeting of the Middlesbrough Circuit by the Revd. Philip Fowler, and there was unanimous approval. Thomas found preaching had taken up his whole time and he preached that sinners should be converted and he taught entire sanctification as the goal for every born-again believer. This caused friction of opinion and some Methodists were not of his opinion. From Wesley's day to the times of the Southport Convention, it has been impossible to proclaim full salvation without rousing opposition and those not in favour usually came from one's own household. Thomas preached a trial sermon to the district meeting and he declared that the blood of Jesus had cleansed him from all sin. As he came to the end of his preaching, he urged people to come forward to receive the blessing. The committee

---

[4]   Henry Smart, *Thomas Cook's Early Ministry*, pp.34-41.

was satisfied with the examination but the sermon he preached was not deemed satisfactory and received low marks. His offering was not acceptable and the July Committee did not recommend him to the Conference.

After his rejection Thomas held a mission at New Marske with Revd. Edward Davidson and the result was that about thirty or forty converts were the visible results of the preacher's labours. In November 1880, the Revd. Joseph Bush, then the chairman of the Halifax and Bradford District, wrote to Thomas and offered him the appointment of lay evangelist to his district. He thought it a wise move and he accepted it on November 21, 1880. He began his mission in the Manningham Circuit, Bradford and services were held every night and Thomas had the joy of showing a large number of converts the way of the Kingdom. Another mission followed at Linthwaite, near Huddersfield, and their converts were recognised as members of the Wesleyan Methodist Church. Then it was on to the Low Moor Circuit, Bradford, and as many as a hundred persons entered the inquiry-rooms on the same evening and for many evenings. Thomas Cook prevailed because of his God-given power of his sole attraction. How true are these sentences from the pen of William Arthur's, *The Tongue of Fire*:

> The converting power is also the only means whereby Christianity raises up agents for her own propagation. That which is wanted in an agent, above all, is zeal – zeal for God, burning desire to save sinners. It is 'Christ in you.' It is 'the love of Christ of constraining you.' It is the Divine nature, which delights to communicate, to bestow, to purify, to save, breathed into the soul of man, and impelling it in the same course wherein Christ Himself moved.... Nothing so re-animates the zeal of old Christians as witnessing the joy and simplicity, the gratitude and fervour, of those who have been lately born of God. It is also wonderful how much the occurrence of conversions heightens the efficiency of men already employed in the ministry, or in other departments of the work of God. The preacher preaches with new heart, the exhorter exhorts with revived feeling, he that prays has

double faith and fervour; and the joy of conquest breathes new vigour into all the Lord's host.[5]

The Revd. Joseph Nettleton was in charge of the Manningham Circuit in 1885 and he wrote of Thomas Cook's labours:

> On my appointment to the Circuit, I was greatly impressed with the abiding fruit of a mission that had been held there by the Rev. Thomas Cook some years before. I found whole classes of young people who had been brought to Christ during the mission, and who had been growing in grace from the time of their conversion. They were earnest Christian workers and were ever ready to support me in all kinds of aggressive evangelism, indoors or out of doors. They gathered other young people into the church, and conducted cottage services and open-air services. I found there young people a great help in the Circuit, and several of them became local preachers and evangelists.[6]

Cook's ministry was remarkably owned of God. Many of the churches were quickened, believers were sanctified and many people were brought into the kingdom. During six months it was found that nearly two thousand had been helped and at least three thousand people found peace with God. Edward Davidson was engaged as Cook's colleague and a period of uninterrupted prosperity occurred. Thirty one missions were held and considerably more than three thousand enquiries were reported. Reports tell of saving and sanctification power and the entire reports speak of the consecration of believers as the main sign of Cook's preaching.

In 1882 Thomas Cook was received by the Wesleyan Methodist Conference as a minister on trial and he was appointed to do the work for which God had been calling him. The Revd. Bowden, in the November 1882 *Methodist Recorder*, wrote of him:

> Thomas Cook, who shall act under the direction of the Home Missionary Committee.... but delayed until the providence of God gave the right man to do the work of a Connexional Evangelist. Such a man has been given this year in Thomas Cook, and an important movement

---

[5]   William Arthur, *The Tongue of Fire*, (1856), pp.185, 186.
[6]   Henry Smart, *Thomas Cook's Early Ministry*, p.67.

of aggressive work has been begun, which we hope will greatly extend.... The Methodist preachers were originally a band of evangelists moving to and fro, and waking up the parishes of the land. John Wesley gave them this rule: 'You have nothing to do but to save souls.'.... The spirit of aggression on the ungodliness and sin around us must be maintained in its vigour, or very soon the Church will not be able to hold its own.... Methodism has had a time of chapel building and financial enterprise; we want now a time of chapel filling and good spiritual work, a revival in every Society.[7]

Thomas Cook revelled in his work as a Connexional Evangelist. During the years that intervened he had given work that will stand, and results that call for devout thanksgiving from those most interested in the evangelized of the kingdom. The largest chapels had been placed at his disposal and he had the complete ecclesiastical organisation of Methodism in Britain. Thomas' first mission as the Connexional Evangelist was held in Bristol and all that time was spent in conducting upwards of six hundred adults entering the inquiry-rooms. At the Centenary Chapel, Boston, Lincolnshire, five hundred people sought salvation and nearly three hundred were present and received notes on trial. In 1883 Thomas held a mission in Roath Road Wesleyan Chapel, Cardiff, and on the last Sunday he held a meeting for the converts and above five hundred attended. In Sheffield seven hundred were taken during a ten day crusade and hundreds more were converted while Sheffield was shaken by Thomas Cook.

In, *The Life of Thomas Cook, Evangelist*, by Henry Smart, there appears a tribute by Revd. Whitehead Clegg on meeting Thomas Cook.

I met Mr. Cook first at Wesley Chapel, Liverpool, when I was sixteen years of age. The Revd. Thomas McCullagh was superintendent of our circuit and was much interested in Mr. Cook.... He preached on the subject of Entire Sanctification, of which he himself was an embodiment. The effect was that all worldliness of the Church was entirely killed, and all the departments were filled with soul-saving

---

[7] Henry Smart, *Thomas Cook's Early Ministry*, pp.72-74.

preachers, teachers and other workers. Thomas Cook's heart-searching addresses and powerful appeals led literally hundreds of persons into a vestry where they sought salvation. The old class-leaders and praying men and women were overwhelmed with what they saw and heard. Ministers and parents wept for joy.... Many were in tears. Several stood up in proof of their desire for a fuller Christian life, and during silent prayer some found what they had sought.... The whole congregation was moved and much blessing rested upon the address. In private his conversation was always uplifting; he never condescended to frivolous matters. He lived in the heavenly places with Christ Jesus, and always brought his friends into the same element. Though he never passed through the Theological Institution, he received a training and schooling of priceless worth.[8]

Thomas was helped by many books and the time came when he could offer his own production. He called it, *Looking Unto Jesus: First Steps In The Way Of Life*, and it turned out to be a best-seller. It opens with three questions; 'Am I Really Converted?', 'The Life of Simple Faith in Christ', and, 'How to Keep Religion When we get it'. Dealing with the third principle, Thomas sets out a counsel.

To keep from sinning is the main idea. We are kept by the power of God through faith. And real true faith is nothing but man's weakness leaning upon God's strength. Our faith links our weakness to God's Omnipotence. On the first approach of temptation, we must learn to fly at once to the 'cleft of the Rock.' If clouds of adversity gather round you, if you are surprised into sin and your heart condemns you, whatever your circumstances, at all times, and everywhere, 'looking unto Jesus' must be the attitude of your souls. Sheep do not take care of the shepherd: the shepherd keeps the sheep. We are safe so long as we commit the whole responsibility of the keeping of our souls to Christ. 'None shall be able to pluck them out of my Father's hand' (John 10:29).[9]

Next Thomas Cook deals with 'Sources of Strength'; prayer, reading the Bible, Christian work and Christian fellowship. Thomas knew

---

8   Henry Smart, *The Life of Thomas Cook, Evangelist*, (1913), pp.93-95.
9   Thomas Cook, *Looking Unto Jesus: First Steps In The Way Of Life*, (1892), pp.9, 10.

that Methodists would be sure of buying these booklets and he had a word for those under Christian fellowship.

> If you have decided to become Methodists, it will be necessary for you to join one of our Society Classes. These are select meetings for social spiritual intercourse, and undeniably most helpful. Under the leadership of some person of experience, a number of Christians meet together once a week, to help each other to live according to the Gospel; and this, by prayer, fellowship, and spiritual counsel. Multitudes gratefully testify to the unspeakable benefit and blessing they have received from the Class-meeting.[10]

Lastly, Thomas Cook deals with 'General Counsels', and he has four proposals in hand; 'Be careful in the choice of your companions', 'Questionable things', 'Grow in grace' and, 'Be bright'. Under the second heading, 'Questionable things', he has the following:

> If you have never begun to smoke, do not begin. Some professing Christians spend more money in tobacco than they give to God. It is an unseemly, unnecessary, unhealthy, and unpleasant habit. It is unnatural, also, and men have to force nature before they can enjoy it. I do not say it is a sin to smoke; though it would be a sin to me, because my conscience condemns it.... As to strong drink, it hardly comes under the head of 'questionable things.' It is undoubtedly an evil, and ought to be renounced. For the sake of these weaker ones, I beseech you abstain altogether. It does seem to me that every Christian should give up that which is ruining so many precious souls, some of them in our own families. I am a teetotaller for the sake of others. For the sake of those for whom Christ died, will you not follow my example?[11]

Under the section, 'Grow in grace', Thomas has something for every reader.

> God's purpose is to exclude all sin from our hearts, that there may be nothing in us at all contrary to pure love. And when love fills our hearts, we shall be in possession of all the graces of the Holy Spirit without their opposites in any degree. This deliverance from heart-sin is what we Methodists call 'entire sanctification.' In my case, it was a definite, distinct experience, as really so as my conversion. As every

---

[10] Thomas Cook, *Looking Unto Jesus: First Steps In The Way Of Life*, p.20.
[11] Thomas Cook, *Looking Unto Jesus: First Steps In The Way Of Life*, pp.25, 26.

road in England points to London, so in the Bible everything points to holiness. The memories of our Methodist fathers will stir your hearts. When I read them the spark of desire in my heart was fanned into a mighty flame. I felt what God had done for them, He could do for me. May the mantle of Stoner, Bramwell, and Collins fall upon the reader of these words. [12]

Thomas was more than pleased when he learned that selling the tracts amounted to half a million copies. He was only twenty-six when he produced his first tract and he had a way of writing that attracted thousands upon thousands. From his first production Thomas was keen to promote Scriptural holiness and he kept that up in all his writings. He was a Methodist and he embraced holiness of life in the way the Scripture taught him.

Cornwall has always been Methodist country and in 1883 it was filled with Methodist people. When Thomas made Cornwall his stamping ground, he was at first taken by surprise because of his youth, but as time passed, he was taken on and held in high esteem by those Cornish Methodists. At Camborne the results were marvellous.

> About half-a-dozen found peace with God that night and the successes of the mission was insured. The next evening the number of converts was larger; the following evening it was larger still, and so the work continued to spread.... Never has the Evangelist laboured with a more loyal and devoted people. Soon the spacious chapel became too small for the congregation even on the week-evenings. Often was it crowded an hour before the time when the service was announced to begin, and a messenger was sent to the preacher's home asking him to go at once and begin the service, as it was useless to keep the crowd waiting in the chapel. It is impossible adequately to describe what took place in the wonderful Camborne mission.... Not seldom the service would last from six o'clock to eleven o'clock and it was hard to get the people to leave. When the Spirit of the Lord is copiously poured out, coldness and conventionalities are destroyed, and the sacred fire begins to burn. [13]

---

[12] Thomas Cook, *Looking Unto Jesus: First Steps In The Way Of Life*, pp.27-29.
[13] Henry Smart, *Thomas Cook's Early Ministry*, pp.204-207.

Methodism has reason to be proud of what happened in the larger chapels in Cornwall – Redruth, Falmouth, Truro and Penzance, and Thomas saw it all on this wonderful crusade. Also in its smaller chapels; while the country is dotted with Wesleyan chapels; and the people flock there to attend church. Thomas Cook saw this in those larger chapels and he knew that in the smaller chapels there were people who worshipped there and longed for a revival that would turn the tide.

Tiviot Dale Chapel, Stockport, was the next place to invite Cook and in 1884 it was the scene of a gracious visitation, of which the Revd. J. D. Stevens comments:

> Never since Tiviot Dale Chapel was built have such scenes been witnessed in it as were seen during Mr. Cook's mission. The congregation steadily increased as the mission proceeded. During the first week the chapel, large as it is, was for the most part well filled. But from the second Sunday the place was all too small; and from some of the services hundreds had to go away, there being no room for them.... At the close of the mission it was found that the names of seven hundred and forty adults and four hundred children had been taken in the inquiry-room.... But perhaps the most extraordinary of all the meetings were those for men only, held in the afternoons of the second and third Sundays. To see the large chapel filled in every part with men, and especially to see the large number that went into the inquiry-rooms was a sight never to be forgotten. The work in the inquiry-rooms was most interesting; almost every variety of case and character presented itself there.... In addition to all the rest, and as important as all the rest, the mission has resulted in a quickened Church.[14]

From Stockport, Thomas went to West Bromwich where he held a mission which was held in a spacious Wesleyan Chapel. The building was filled and at the men's meeting sixteen hundred were present and many of them yielded themselves to Christ. Reports of this mission state that one thousand and forty-eight persons had professed to find peace with God during Thomas's preaching. Walsall is a

---

[14] Henry Smart, *Thomas Cook's Early Ministry*, pp.87, 88.

neighbouring town to West Bromwich, and again Cook's fervent evangelism was the key. On the last evening, congregations numbered three thousand and the converts numbered nine hundred.

Another large mission was held about this time at Pendleton, in the Irwell Street Circuit, Manchester. The Revd. George Walker was then Superintendent of the Circuit and his report makes exciting reading.

> During the first week the congregations increased each evening, and four hundred persons above fourteen years of age professed decision. The second Sunday commenced with a remarkable service at seven am. About six hundred were present, including nearly all who had found Christ during the previous week, and others who had received answers to prayer in the salvation of friends.... The service for men only, in the afternoon, was most impressive. About fifteen hundred men were present, nearly fifty of whom decided for Christ.... In the evening the crowd was almost awful; the interior of the spacious building presented the sight of one mass of living beings all bowed down under the power of God.... The total number of converts exceeded eleven hundred, of whom more than half belonged to other places of worship.... The people are crowding the classes; numbers who did not go into the inquiry-rooms are joining the Church. The band-meetings and prayer-meetings are attended by hundreds.[15]

The mission which Thomas Cook conducted at Oldham was a testimony to the drawing power of God. The second Sunday was a day never to be forgotten. In the afternoon the chapel was crowded with men and nearly fifteen hundred were present and a good number responded to Cook. At the evening service hundreds were unable to get in to the chapel and the names of about seven hundred and fifty inquirers were taken. The sons and daughters of some of their leading members, long prayed for, have been brought to God. Thomas Cook was still a young man and to the joy of many, preached to get young people to the altar. He was a youthful evangelist and perhaps the youth were particularly drawn to him. But he never slacked in his

---

[15] Henry Smart, *Thomas Cook's Early Ministry*, pp.92, 93.

purpose and Methodism could and did encourage all people, young and old, to attend his service.

Later on he held a mission in Portsmouth and before he started, men and women who were assured that he was the right man, covenanted together to fast and pray that God would intervene in this campaign. The Revd. Richard Hardy gives thanks for what the Lord has done in this city of many temptations.

> The evening services were crowded and Pentecostal blessing resulted. Those who never entered God's house, as well as the unsaved who frequented it, were awakened and converted. Drunkards, wrestling with their foe as in a death struggle, gave up the drink, and on their knees sought the Saviour.... These converts still retain the blessing they then found and revivals that bear such fruit are reminded that which was done in Ephesus when the convicted burned their books, are done today when people 'burn their bridges' and start afresh with the power of God. So mightily grew the Word of God and prevailed.[16]

Thomas Cook visited Ireland and he gathered a crowd around him when he preached in Dublin. The services were crowded with many Roman Catholics being among the hearers. The names of seven hundred inquirers were taken and the people were blessed and strengthened in their faith. A report in a Dublin newspaper gives the facts.

> Mr. Cook is one of the best evangelists of this generation. His sermons are not remarkable for eloquence, originality, or thoughtfulness. They are remarkable for plain, pointed, earnest appeals. The interest never flags, the great question of present decision for God is never lost sight of, and all through there is an unction from the Holy One. His management of a meeting is beyond praise. His ready tact, his power of command, his tender sympathy, give constant opportunities for wonder and delight. The principal cause of success is found in the afternoon meetings for holiness. Here Mr. Cook is seen at his best. His clear views, his telling illustrations, his powerful appeals at these meetings, can never be forgotten. A new life seems to be before Methodism in Dublin.[17]

---

[16] Henry Smart, *Thomas Cook's Early Ministry*, pp.97, 98.
[17] Henry Smart, *Thomas Cook's Early Ministry*, p.100.

In March 1889, Thomas Cook visited Leeds and held a mission in the historic Brunswick Chapel. During the course of the mission, five hundred adults found salvation and the holiness services were well attended. A ministerial correspondent writes of this Brunswick mission.

> One thing is clear: the old-fashioned truth, simply and earnestly preached in the old-fashioned Methodist way, has still a charm for the people, and is still blessed of God to the salvation of souls. We had eighteen services in ten days. In Mr. Cook's sermons there is no mere intellectual effect, no modern thought, but, instead, there is deep and earnest warning, close and powerful wrestling with the conscience and with the will, and solemn appeal. Some of his sermons were to me like an echo of those which I used to hear in my boyhood, and which have been, alas, too scarce in modern years. But it is under these sermons that men and women are awakened, and led to decision for God. Oh, for more of such preaching, and for more of the divine power to accompany the Word.[18]

From the reports of Thomas Cook's services, the facts are that in many places, the work was so mighty that Thomas saw it as the work of the Lord. Every year the work was growing stronger and he felt that it was down to divine intervention. In the years of 1886 and 1887, he visited places of which no mention has been made; Skipton, Birmingham, Bradford, Leek, Gainsborough, Leicester, Launceston, and Zetland were among the number. Thomas entered upon this work with fear and trembling, for he was young, inexperienced and without much resource. The ministers of the various places received him gladly and were determined to have a mission attracting thousands. Thomas has publicly said that in the beginning of his work, he had, as it were, five loaves and two small fish. He presented these to his Lord and great has been the blessing wherever he went.

Thomas made a visit to Cambridge and spoke to the young men there of Full Salvation. He published it in a penny booklet with the title, *Full Salvation: A Talk to Undergraduates*. He speaks of the Cambridge visit and of the response he had to their invitation.

---

[18]   Henry Smart, *Thomas Cook's Early Ministry*, pp.101, 102.

The meeting was most impressive and memorable; none of us will ever forget how the glory of the Lord filled the place as we bowed before Him, waiting for the sanctifying fire. The presence of God was so near and so real that for some time we were scarcely conscious of anything else. A strange sacred awe preceded a season of indescribable sweetness, which so permeated our souls that for the moment we seemed to be swallowed up in the great deep of the divine presence and power. It was pre-eminently a season of grace and delight; many of us date a new era in our religious life from that sacred hour. We could not do otherwise than believe that God had taken full possession of our hearts.[19]

On June 28, 1888, aged twenty-nine, Thomas Cook married Mary Ann Dawson, the daughter of Joshua Dawson. The marriage was a short one, for in October, 1889, his first and only child was born, and in the following February, 1890, Mary Ann died, and Thomas was left with a young child. One night as he was praying, pleading with God to sooth his troubled spirit, he was answered by a message to this effect: Infinite Love, Infinite Wisdom, Infinite Power. He rose from his knees, praised God for the consolation and henceforth was kept in peace whenever a problem beset him. He remained a widower for four years, and then on January 10, 1894, he married Jessie Foster of Ripon. This union lasted for nineteen years and she was a joy to Thomas Cook during his mission and finally his years as the first Principal of Cliff College in Derbyshire.

In 1886 Thomas Cook went to Norway and held evangelistic services and his friend, Dr. Wood of Southport, accompanying him. There were three thousand five hundred members, three thousand Sunday School scholars and thirty three ministers. Methodism was introduced into Norway by a Norwegian sailor named Pedersen. He returned to America, sought ordination and returned to Norway. A Norwegian minister happened to be in Cardiff when Thomas Cook held a mission there and he urged the evangelist to visit Norway on an evangelistic tour. Thomas was fortunate in securing an interpreter who knew both Norwegian and English. He was moved when he saw

[19] Henry Smart, *The Life of Thomas Cook, Evangelist*, p.80.

his Norwegian hearers praying with tearful faces. Truly the city of God which lies foursquare has twelve gates and Thomas Cook's career is an illustration of that truth. We see him here triumphing in Christ in Norway as he had done in the United Kingdom. Later on we shall see him in South Africa among the Dutch, Ceylon in the Sinhalese and Tamil Circuits, and then in Australia and New Zealand among the Maoris.

Six years after his visit to Norway, he was invited to visit the South African Conference. He began his South African tour in April, 1892, and finished it in November. He wrote of it in a book, *My Mission Tour in South Africa: A Record of Interesting Travel and Pentecostal Blessing*, and it was produced in 1893. He went to Port Elizabeth and the local paper published his address.

> The Rev. Thomas Cook, having taken his place on the platform at the request of the President, said he had hoped to avoid that occasion, as it was more to his mind to do the work than to talk about it. His coming to the country represented the deep interest the home Church took in the work and welfare of the Church in South Africa.... Two things he would say at once – he believed in God, and he believed in his mission.... They must deal with truth and duty, with sin and its penalty. They must use the law as the knife to wound, and then pour the oil of the gospel into the wound. The doctrine of sanctification must be preached; Methodism teaching was full on this subject. The Southport Convention had attracted much attention to it in England. It was the chief end for which Methodism was raised up.... Above all else, they must seek the baptism of the Holy Ghost. Everything without this availed but little. This, and this only, was essential to the success of Christianity.[20]

Thomas Cook goes on to describe how the Town Hall was secured and it took nearly one thousand people. From the first service to the last, they had full and enthusiastic congregations and the power of God was upon every service. Thomas enthusiastically reports:

> Souls were saved in every service, and the blessing increased daily. Whole families sought and found the Saviour. Strong men wept in

---

[20] Thomas Cook, *My Mission Tour in South Africa*, (1893), pp.11, 12.

humble contrition, old people obtained forgiveness, and young men and maidens dedicated their lives to God. The effect of the mission was to thoroughly arouse the town.... Our last service was especially a season of grace and delight. Some who were under conviction of sin had written during the day to ask me to be sure and give another invitation that night, as they wanted to confess Christ. When I did so, the response was such that we had the greatest difficulty in finding workers and accommodation for the number who came. Few who were present will ever forget the solemnity and holy influence of that occasion. Altogether during the mission two hundred and thirty persons were helped in the inquiry-rooms, but many received Christ in their seats who afterwards expressed a desire to join themselves to His people.... Several others were converted the Sabbath after the mission, and when reports were received later, the work was still going on. The effect of such a beginning was unspeakable blessed in relation to the other fields of labour which I subsequently visited. Desire and prayer were encouraged, and faith abundantly increased.[21]

Johannesburg is situated two hundred and fifty miles from Bloemfontein which Thomas had heard so much about and he immediately opted for it. On his arrival, Revd. Appelbe, the Superintendent Minister, who had stood at his side at Didsbury College, Manchester, ten years before when Cook was examined as a candidate for the ministry, received him with his accustomed geniality, and gave him, in Irish, *Cael mela faltha*, - 'a hundred thousand welcomes' – to the Goal Fields.

Our church not being large enough to accommodate the crowds we expected, the circus, which is the largest building in the town, was engaged for the occasion. At least eighteen hundred persons assembled to listen to my message on the Sunday night.... Many stood up in the presence of the huge assembly to confess their decision to serve God, and came out and knelt at chairs provided for enquirers, that they might publicly dedicate their lives to God. The exact number of conversions we found it impossible to secure, as we had no vestry and no communion rail to which we could invite those who were seeking. Eight-five adults gave in their names who had professed to receive Christ as their Saviour, but many others were blessed whose names we

---

[21] Thomas Cook, *My Mission Tour in South Africa*, pp.17-20.

could not obtain. Altogether it was a most enjoyable visit, and so full of blessing that I was extremely reluctant to be obliged to leave after the third day.[22]

Thomas Cook moved on to Queenstown which is essentially English and the Methodism there was more like Cook always enjoyed. The Methodist Church there was capable of seating eight hundred people and the total membership was around one hundred and fifty.

> We had the best beginning at Queenstown of any place I had visited up to that date. More than ninety decided for Christ the first Sabbath, of whom sixty-six were above fourteen years of age. Each night afterwards, increased power seemed to be given with the Truth, until the communion rail was far too small to accommodate those who were anxious to be saved. It filled the heart of God's people with devout thanksgiving, to see nearly all the grown-up sons and daughters of our Methodist people in the town solemnly and publicly avowing their decision for Christ. Almost every variety of case and character presented itself among the inquirers, and no less than two hundred and thirty persons professed to find peace with God.... On the second Sabbath afternoon, a service was held for the natives at the location, which produced a deep and lasting impression. Every square foot of space on the building was crowded, while round the doors and windows stood disappointed groups for whom there was no room in the church. The upturned faces, smiles, tears, distorted features and trembling limbs, told of mental and emotional pressure which could not for long be restrained. And so it proved. We had no sooner finished than the whole congregation seemed to break down. Their pent-up feelings gave vent, and cries for mercy filled the place. Not only were the rail and the seats in front filled with seekers, but in all parts of the building men and women were weeping and piteously pleading with God for the pardon of their sins. This is but a glimpse of the indescribable scenes of that service.[23]

King William's Town lies about forty miles from East London and this was Thomas Cook's next visit. The Wesleyan Church not being large enough for the mission services, the Presbyterian Church was

22 Thomas Cook, *My Mission Tour in South Africa*, pp.40-44.
23 Thomas Cook, *My Mission Tour in South Africa*, pp.61-63.

placed at their disposal. The town was a centre of cliques and divisions and that was reckoned a place hard to get decisions. The result was marvellous as Thomas reports:

> The first Sabbath over forty conversions were reported, but this was followed by a hardness for three or four week-nights, which we could not understand, and which none could explain. This continued until the Friday night, when prayer and faith prevailed. The hardness melted before the Spirit's genial influences, and that night we had a real old-fashioned breakdown. Before the mission closed, over two hundred persons came out on the Lord's side. At the close of the service, about thirty persons of various ages sought forgiveness of sins. In the after meeting I noticed the native minister was weeping and apparently in much distress. On asking the cause of it, he pointed to an old man kneeling among the seekers, and said, 'That is my father. We have tried for thirty years to win him for Christ, but he has two wives, and has been unwilling until now to renounce the younger one. Now he says he is willing to sell all to obtain the pearl of great price.'[24]

The next place was Annshaw and it was the only place where Cook conducted a native circuit through an interpreter. He took time to explain it all to the schoolmaster, explaining it all and emphasising the points he wished to make clear. But he need not have bothered for the Holy Ghost was present and everything was in order.

> A strange joy possessed me as a thousand dusky faces looked into my face with eager longing for the word of life. Failure was out of the question - God was with me, and that was enough. It was an audience such as I had waited for years, to confirm again the theory I have always held, that it is possible to preach the gospel, even to heathen, with saving power through an interpreter. After singing and prayer, the text was announced, and for about an hour I reason with them 'of righteousness, temperance, and judgment to come,' addressing myself almost entirely to the understanding, the conscience, and the will. Profound silence reigned during the sermon, but tearful eyes and distorted features indicated the keen piercing of the Spirit's sword. This developed into suppressed sobbing and smothered cries for mercy during silent prayer; but when we commenced to sing, they could control themselves no longer. One after another, men and women,

---

[24] Thomas Cook, *My Mission Tour in South Africa*, pp.74, 75.

hurried out to the communion rail, broken down and penitent, until the scene presented was one never to be forgotten. They were now all praying audibly, and the floor was wet with tears; such sighs and groans, such prostration, such agony of soul are rarely seen in England. Eighty souls that day professed to find remission of sins, among them several Europeans and not a few heathen.[25]

Cook was inspired to say that one of Chief Kama's councillors was among the seekers and his conversion caused great joy. He was not only a man of considerable influence but of substance. He had held out for thirty years, boasting that he was a heathen, but sitting under Cook's ministry, he gave in and a few days after he brought the interpreter and gave his conversion story. Two of his brothers also found the Lord and a woman who had on thirty-five rings now told him that she had put on the Lord Jesus Christ and there was no room for the rings. Thomas tells us that from the second Sabbath, there was no room in the church and he conducted the service in the open air.

It was a gathering such as in the history of the tribe had never been known before. Trusting to the immediate presence and saving power of the Holy Spirit, we commenced the service. A strange solemnity rested upon us from the beginning, which deepened into an awful sense of the presence of God and melting power as the service went on. About half-way through the sermon the pent-up emotions of the people gave vent and cries for mercy rent the air. Some fell as dead and had to be carried to the front. Others staggered forward, literally roaring in disquietude of soul, and on reaching the church they seemed for a time to be in a state of utter collapse. Sobs, sighs, and groans were heard on every side. Nothing that I have before witnessed so reminded me of what is recorded of the day of Pentecost. Altogether on the second Sabbath alone, about four hundred persons came forward as anxious inquirers, nearly all of whom professed to realise God's forgiving love. The next day was very similar, one hundred and fifty names were taken, making the total of those who sought salvation during the mission over nine hundred.[26]

---

[25] Thomas Cook, *My Mission Tour in South Africa*, pp.82-85.
[26] Thomas Cook, *My Mission Tour in South Africa*, pp.85, 86.

Leaving Annshaw, Thomas visited Grahamstown and was put up by the Revd. Theophilus Chubb and was treated there to make Grahamstown one of the most enjoyable of the whole series. The mission having been long and eagerly anticipated and the people there in readiness, not only the missioner but the people were in ready response.

> We had crowded congregations at all three services on the first Sabbath, and before the day was over more than one hundred persons above fourteen years of age had come forward to the communion rail to declare their decision to serve God. The increased interest was evidenced by the congregations becoming larger as the days passed, and the growing power of the services, from the fact, not only that we had more inquirers, but the older members of the congregation began to yield themselves to God. Whole families were among the seekers, husbands with their wives, nearly all the choir, and scores of young men. On one or two occasions there came a real old-fashioned breakdown, when, in a few moments after my sermon, the spacious communion rail was more than filled, and I was obliged to request others who were anxious to remain in their seats until accommodation could be provided for them. The afternoon holiness meetings were largely attended, and much blessed in the deepening and quickening of the spiritual life of the Church. Many Christians re-dedicated themselves to God, and some sought and found that 'perfect love' which 'casteth out fear.'[27]

Thomas Cook moved on to Cradock, about one hundred miles from Grahamstown and the mission was held in the Dutch Reformed Church which sat twelve hundred people. The mission commenced with an early morning prayer meeting and flocks of people attended and took part.

> We received at that service the earnest of the coming blessing. Splendid congregations assembled all day, especially at the evening meeting. A gracious power was present which drove the word deep into the hearts of those who listened. My subject was the danger of destroying spiritual receptivity; and at the close of the sermon the inquiry-rooms were filled with those who were anxious to be saved. Each night during the week the services were continued, and as usual,

---

[27] Thomas Cook, *My Mission Tour in South Africa*, p.103.

the interest and power greatly increased as the end of the mission drew nigh. One of the local papers said: 'Mr. Cook's naturalness, his manly and eloquent diction and intense earnestness, won the hearts of all. Gifted with the power of persuasion, and with a manner ever bright and cheerful, he allures to brighter worlds and leads the way. But he can be stern. Scathingly does he denounce sin. Vividly does he bring the past of men's lives before them, and firmly does he insist upon the truth that the past must be forgiven ere a new life can be begun.'[28]

He left Cradock early in the morning and reached Somerset East in time for the afternoon service. The town is about fourteen miles from the railway station and he found a good congregation gathered, consisting of members of the various churches.

In the evening the Town Hall was engaged for the services and standing room only could be obtained. The greater proportion of those present remained to the after-meeting, and many occupied the front seats in evidence of their desire to accept Christ. To those I explained the way of salvation, praying with and for them. The earnestness which reigned in quietness was most notable, and several believed unto salvation.

Somerset East is the place where our late venerated friend, the Rev. Alexander M'Aulay, died, and is buried. I was much pleased with the appropriate orderliness which marked his resting-place, and thought, as I looked around the little cemetery, what a lovely spot it was in which to wait for the resurrection morn. A neat stone has been erected, with a suitable inscription, and beneath his name the words, which were never better applied, 'Faithful unto death.' Standing in view of his finished course, I could not but bless God for so worthy and fruitful a life; and I prayed that I might hand down to others an example of unswerving loyalty to Jesus Christ, and sustained enthusiasm for the salvation of souls, such as he has done. Though he laboured but a few months in this country, his name is revered among all classes of people almost as much as it is in England.[29]

Durban is the seaport of the Colony and Thomas arrived there to conduct his mission. For spiritual activity and vigorous life, Durban

---

[28] Thomas Cook, *My Mission Tour in South Africa*, pp.109, 110.
[29] Thomas Cook, *My Mission Tour in South Africa*, p.115.

Methodism compared favourably with any of the half-dozen of best churches at home. The preparation for the mission were most thorough and complete and no expense was spared to make it a go. For months the mission had been devoutly anticipated and the week before Thomas's arrival, the whole Circuit united in prayer to seek power from on high.

> The access God gave us to the people was very remarkable. On the first Sabbath rain fell steadily all day but ours was filled at all the services. At the close of the first week it was found that two hundred and fifty persons had entered the inquiry-rooms. On the Sunday the rain began to fall, but nothing could keep the people away from the church; every available space was occupied and numbers remained standing wherever they could hear. It was a season of glorious triumph; more than ninety that day decided to serve God. On Monday and Tuesday the same scenes were repeated, only that the inquiry-rooms were not large enough. Hence the spacious communion rail was also filled with inquirers.... The place was packed with natives and twelve hundred at least attended the service, mostly heathen Zulus, and wonderful results followed. Two or three rows knelt behind these, and all the aisles were filled, until I was compelled once more to ask that all others who were anxious should remain in their seats and seek the Lord there. That day was a red-letter day among the days of power which I witnessed in South Africa. To God be all the praise for ever.... My visit to Natal will rank among the most precious experiences of my life. The thought of it will be one of my pleasantest memories. When I left Maritzburg, many assembled at the station to bid me farewell, and, as the train moved away from the platform, sang for me the familiar prayer:
>
> > God be with you till we meet again
> > By His counsels guide, uphold you
> > With His sheep securely fold you
> > God be with you till we meet again.[30]

Thomas left Maritzburg on Wednesday, October 19, 1892, and he reached Johannesburg. When he arrived he found a telegram announcing his arrival at the service. When he turned to the paper, he found a caption headed, *Cook the Converter*, followed by a lengthy

---

[30] Thomas Cook, *My Mission Tour in South Africa*, pp.126-136.

account of his service at Maritzburg, concluding with an account of his leaving and people wished him 'God-speed'. At Cape Town he learned from one of the ministers that they had a week of prayer and were now ready to meet him. They were expecting showers of blessing and there was a heightening expectancy.

From the first service until the last, two thousand men and women crowded into the beautiful Metropolitan Church. Such power accompanied the word and the vestries were far too small to accommodate the inquirers. The results filled the hearts of God's people with gratitude and there was no less than six hundred and fifty-five persons came out on the Lord's side.... The saintly Andrew Murray sat with me on the platform and assisted in the inquiry-room on several occasions.... Our holiness meetings attracted much notice and the meetings were well attended. Some beautiful testimonies were received and there be no doubt but that higher service caused the people to respond. We had prayed that the last mission might be the best and in some respects the experience at Cape Town exceeded all others. The tide of spiritual influence seemed to rise higher at the last service than on any previous occasion. Hundreds were turned away who could not get into the building and the rush for seats when the door was opened was more like a pantomime than anything else. God did indeed bless the mission, and eternity only will reveal the result.

My mission at Cape Town closed on November 8th, and a host of friends came down to wish me God-speed on the journey. Messages and telegrams reached me on the dock and I can hear them saying, 'Queenstown friends wish you safe and pleasant voyage,' 'Loving farewell from Maritzburg,' 'Glad congratulations on grand results,' 'Our hearty prayers for your future,' 'Cradock prays God's blessing be with you.' And sometimes I fancy that I still hear the hymn which they sung:

> Shall we gather at the river?
> The beautiful, beautiful river
> Shall we gather at the river?
> That flows by the throne of God.[31]

Thomas had spent six months in South Africa and he conducted two hundred and twenty services at which six thousand sought the Lord

---
[31] Thomas Cook, *My Mission Tour in South Africa*, pp.140-143.

and many more were blessed. God had used him in a most remarkable way and there was no more trouble about God using him in the future.

Thomas reached home in York and on January 10, 1894, he was married to Jessie Foster of Markenfield Hall, near Ripon, and for nineteen years she actively co-operated with him in all his evangelistic tours. In one of his books, *Days of God's Right Hand*, (1896), he tells of his experiences in four years of travel in Australia, New Zealand and Ceylon. He writes:

> To make sure of impartial reports, as far as I could secure them, written by resident ministers, describing the work in their own churches.... My use of the plural numbers includes my wife who was my companion in travel and toil... When the late Mr. Joshua Dawson, of Weardale, was dying, he told certain members of his family that the conviction had grown upon him, during his illness, that I should be sent to the ends of the earth to do the work of an evangelist. This, from such a man, at such a time, coupled with similar impressions of my own, prepared me to respond favourably to the invitation of the South Australian Methodist Conference to conduct missions in various parts of Australia.... The valedictory meetings, held in the Exeter Hall, London, a few days before we sailed, filled us with larger hopes, and inspired new courage with which to face the responsibilities of our undertaking. It was pre-eminently a season of grace and delight, and furnished encouragement afterwards, when we were far away, in times of difficulty and temptation.[32]

Thomas started with a service in Albany because he believed that a revived Church is the first great need. He spoke about the Pentecostal baptism and that made the church the indispensable condition of success. At night the building was crowded and God gave the first fruits of the harvest He was going to send in Australia. At Perth he preached with great power in a crowded church and the Lord came down in blessing. The spreading flame reached adjacent townships and the whole area was revived.

---

[32] Thomas Cook, *Days of God's Right Hand*, (1896), pp.5-13.

The church has been quickened, backsliders have been recovered, while others have been claimed from sin and shame. A spirit of hopefulness has sprung up in the hearts of the members. Some are seeking the fullness of the Spirit, others are pressing into the land of perfect love. Holiness meetings were largely attended and greatly blessed. Two hundred souls God gave us at Perth represent more than will appear at first sight. Taking into consideration the religious condition of the colony, the limited population, and the fact that we are only nine days in the city, the ministers thought the results were cause for profoundest gratitude to God and remarkable as exceeding the expectations of the most sanguine. The membership of this Church was largely augmented, and most of the other churches shared in the benefit.... The Church is prospering on all lines and 'the best of all, God is with us.' our name and work with us are sweet and helpful memories.[33]

Thomas and Jessie travelled to Kent Town Church and the Revd. James Haslam, from Bolton in Lancashire, was the pastor. He made arrangements for Thomas to come to Australia and he was glad that he had booked them.

The result was that congregations were all that we could desire. A large number of seekers entered the inquiry-rooms and night by night the power and interest increased until the Sabbath, when the spacious church was far too small to accommodate the crowds that came to hear. Friday nights were set apart for holiness meetings, on which occasions the congregations were larger than on any other night. The hunger for instructions on this subject was most inspiring, and the number who received definite blessing was not the last important result of our visit. Conversions multiplied so rapidly that before the end of the mission, between four and five hundred persons had professed to receive remission of sins. Noonday prayer-meetings were largely attended. At the last service the church was a spectacle never to be forgotten. Aisles and passages were crowded and doorways thronged. But the most interesting sight was that of new converts, who filled the central area from the communion rail to the rear of the church, and though two thousand voices made the wall vibrate to the foundations, the song which most affected the ear and heart was the doxology when

---

[33]   Thomas Cook, *Days of God's Right Hand*, pp.36, 37.

sung alone by the four hundred and eighty souls who had been brought to religious decision during the mission.[34]

In the following months Thomas and Jessie travelled to Moonta, Kardina, Kooringa, Port Pirie and the Broken Hill Circuits. More than two thousand persons had professed conversions and a large number had received the Holy Ghost. In each Circuit the song of salvation continued to be sung by a constantly increasing company of the saved.

> To Mr. Cook the meeting desires to tender its warmest thanks; to acknowledge its great admiration of, and to bless God for, his singleness of purpose and his untiring zeal in labour incessant. His coming has been to our own and other churches a timely lesson, and a sowing from which is expected an abiding harvest of good. To Mrs. Cook, his devoted wife, and true help-meet in this sacred work, the meeting respectfully and gratefully proffers its thanks, and prays that both may have the continued protection of Almighty God in their journeyings hence, and that the harvest of their reaping may, under God, be yet more abundant and blessed.[35]

Leaving Adelaide, the Cooks travelled on to Melbourne, a distance of five hundred miles. Their first mission was held in Wesley Church which was pastored by Mr. Edgar who had a congregation of a thousand people. The evening meetings increased proportionately and Thomas saw the Lord move in an extraordinary manner. At least six thousand persons attended on the second Sunday and no less than one hundred and eight professed to find a Saviour. It would be impossible to give more than an outline of other Victorian missions. While in Melbourne Thomas was asked to give a lecture on 'How to preach, so as to save souls', to a Methodist ministers' conference. Thomas stood up and declared what he found in preaching and in people. This was somebody addressing a company of ministers who left school at an early age, and with an incomplete education, who never went to any college, a man whose theological studies to the end of his days were meagre. And yet, this man had won thousands to

---

[34] Thomas Cook, *Days of God's Right Hand*, pp.47, 48.
[35] Thomas Cook, *Days of God's Right Hand*, p.96.

Christ. The range of his ministry was extraordinarily wide and covered the young and the old, the rich and the poor, the ignorant and the learned, as well as all sorts of people in the United Kingdom. The long and the short of it is this: 'The hand of the Lord was with him, and a great number that believed turned to the Lord' (Acts 11:21). As Thomas added:

> Above all, the weakest among us will accomplish more for God than the strongest will without it. What I urge particularly is, that a baptism is a sort of initiatory rite to a life of Pentecostal service. Before we receive our Pentecost there is not much service worth the name. With the promised baptism the apostles entered upon a new phase of life and work. And so it is to-day. Christian life begins at Calvary, but effective service begins with the baptism of fire. These points comprised my address, and were exemplified in the missions I conducted. They are the secret maxims and principles of my life and work; and the longer I live the more am I confirmed in the opinion that God has given me these views in regard to the best method of winning souls. Several who heard, and were helped and blessed, carried the flame to districts we were not able to visit.[36]

Thomas and Jessie moved onwards to Bathurst and in the mission, proved to be a joy to all concerned. The church was packed with people and at one particular service eight men over thirty decided to stand by the Lord and evoked great admiration. During his visit to their assembly, the President asked Thomas to preach. The service was held in the large Centenary Hall which was filled with ministers and laymen.

> My subject was, 'The Pentecostal Baptism,' and God graciously helped me in explaining this to be the indispensable condition of success in Christian work. The mighty victories of the early Church were won in the power of the Holy Ghost. Nobody ever was, or ever will be, saved, only through the preaching of the gospel. It is the gospel applied and enforced by the Holy Spirit that saves men. The work is spiritual, and only spiritual power will accomplish it. The Pentecostal baptism will bring Pentecostal results. God does not hire out His attributes, as some imagine, He comes to our hearts Himself. If we want power we must seek Him, and He will work through us. The apostles had received a

---

[36]   Thomas Cook, *Days of God's Right Hand*, p.128.

measure of the Spirit before Pentecost, but Pentecost made an unspeakable difference. It is one thing to have the Spirit, but quite another to be filled with the Spirit. We claim to be sharers of Pentecostal privileges, but how few possess the Pentecostal power.[37]

The next stop for the Cooks was in New Zealand and their campaign began in the Pitt Street Church, Auckland, on January 20, 1895. It would be impossible to give an account of every convert but there are letters received from converts telling of new light and power and love. The President of the Conference, who attended all the meetings, bears testimony to the same. 'The converts I have seen very clear, and are evidently determined to go the whole way. The effect of the mission is, so far, most beneficial to our town, for which we do praise the Lord.'[38]

From Auckland Cook went on to Wellington and the services were held in Wesley Church, which sat one thousand people. Torrents of rain interfered with the congregations but the church was filled each evening and had seekers coming to enquire about Jesus. A minister wrote a report for the *Advocate*.

The church was crowded – floor, galleries, all. The singing was an inspiration, and at the invitation, men, women, and younger people went into the inquiry-room. Mr. Cook keeps the meeting in his own hands from beginning to end. His voice is resonant and clear and he can lead a hymn as easily as he can preach. Very firm is he in requiring that every one should intelligently and clearly grasp the Lord Jesus as a Saviour. The afternoon meetings for the deepening of the spiritual life were most helpful. The sanctified life, not an unsinning state, but an unsinning condition through a moment-by-moment obedience and trust, was understood and entered into by many as it had not been before. The difference between blamelessness and faultlessness was clearly apprehended, and a fuller surrender made, that the blameless life on earth and the faultless life of heaven might be enjoyed. God's people have taken a higher stand, and some two hundred and thirty have professed conversion. These have been members of different congregations, including Roman Catholics. Over one hundred

---

[37] Thomas Cook, *Days of God's Right Hand*, p.181.
[38] Thomas Cook, *Days of God's Right Hand*, p.211.

belonged to Wesley Church, or have expressed a wish to join that Church. All were happy and in last night's praise this happiness was shown. Our mouths are filled with singing, and our hearts with love and thankfulness.[39]

Leaving Wellington the Cooks moved on to Christchurch, Timaru, Dunedin and New Plymouth in North Island. Thomas wrote:

Night by night during the week, we rejoiced over enlarged congregations and increased seriousness, until the mission became the topic of conversation everywhere. A great impression has undoubtedly been made upon the whole district. On the second Monday, so inclement were the elements but between four and five hundreds came to hear the Word of Life, and a goodly number resolved henceforth to be the Lord's.... After the mission the flame spread in a most wonderful manner. In the town and country places, for weeks afterwards, scarcely a service was held without conversions. Ministers and local preachers had the same experience; wherever they went they saw tears of penitence brightened into tears of joy, and confession of sin followed by hallelujahs of deliverance.[40]

Thomas Cook, in his book, *Days of God's Right Hand*, tells how it was their intention to visit India, but after preaching five hundred and sixty times in Australia, they decided it was not possible on that visit. Instead they headed for Ceylon (now Sri Lanka) and conducted a few missions. He writes:

Our first mission was held at Batticaloa, on the east coast of the island, where Christians are few and far between.... The church was thronged when we entered, with eager, enquiring, curious and scornful souls. My interpreter, Rev. W. H. Walton, a native minister, took his stand at one end of the communion table and with such an interpreter I needed to have no apprehension. As the address proceeded the Divine power increased and profound silence reigned. I spoke of sin and its deserved penalty; but when I told them of the Incarnate God and of His dying love, it was amazing how impassive they became. Some got up and walked out. No notice was taken of their departure, the others sat stolid and immovable as ever. The service closed with an appeal for

[39]   Thomas Cook, *Days of God's Right Hand*, pp.213-217.
[40]   Thomas Cook, *Days of God's Right Hand*, pp.246-248.

immediate decision for Christ but none responded. To create this sense of sin I dealt with the sterner truths of the Word the following night. That evening half-a-score of penitents professed to realise God's pardoning mercy. The work had now thoroughly commenced and our hearts were full of praise. Interest grew until the church was far too small to accommodate those who wished to hear. All castes were represented among the seekers. The highest and lowest stood together at the communion rail, confessing Christ.[41]

The two year mission was now at an end and Thomas was given a letter which was written when they left Batticaloa, and signed by more than two hundred persons, all native except about twelve.

Dear Mr. Cook,

We desire in this, the last service of your mission in Batticaloa, to express to you our own deep sense of gratitude for the blessing which, both as individuals and as a church, we have, by God's grace, received in connection with your visit to us. The Word you have preached has been a living Word; old truths have shone with new light and beauty as you have set them before us; and under your clear and forceful preaching many of us have been led into a richer and fuller enjoyment of the Christian life.... Your visit will be a precious memory to our church, and your name will live in our homes and in our hearts. We earnestly and affectionately invite you to visit us again, and we hope that then once more we shall have the pleasure of welcoming Mrs. Cook, whose presence with you on this arduous mission tour has been an added joy to us all, and an encouragement to Christian enterprise to all the ladies of our church. We beg of you to be the bearer of our very grateful thanks to the Home Mission Committee, the Foreign Missionary Committee, and to the Conference, for permitting you to undertake this mission, and to be yourself the mediator of our request to them, that at an early date you may once more be commissioned to make a prolonged visit to our Ceylon and Indian mission-fields.[42]

Thomas was ending two years of mission work among the Australian, New Zealand and Sri Lanka lands. He had preached five hundred and sixty sermons and now, with this letter of encouragement and

---

[41] Thomas Cook, *Days of God's Right Hand*, pp.303-309.
[42] Thomas Cook, *Days of God's Right Hand*, pp.324, 325.

blessing, Thomas and Jessie were heading back to their own country. At the close of his book, there appears one letter, giving thanks to God and praising Him for all His mercies.

> Our service has not been without blemishes and defects, but God has been pleased so richly to bless it that praise shall be our prevailing note. He alone giveth the increase. The victories of the past are but a pledge and earnest of other victories, grander and more glorious.... All other lights shall wane before the presence of Him who is the Light of the world. The day shall come which shall be signalised by His universal triumph. We may not see it before 'this mortal shall have put on immortality,' but we appreciate the privilege of being permitted to assist in hastening that glorious era.... Of one thing we are perfectly satisfied that the old gospel has lost none of its power. Whatever else has changed in this nineteenth century, the gospel, preached in the power of the Holy Spirit, is the same power it ever was. Rightly experienced, lived, and preached, it will produce the same results as followed its declaration in olden times. We have seen all classes and creeds bow before its force, and have had our lifelong conviction intensified that the old-fashioned reliance upon God and on the power of the gospel is all that is needed to save men to-day, as it was in the early days of Christianity. There is no new method of bringing men to God – the Church must return to first principles. So closes our story of two years of grace. To God and the Lamb be praise for ever![43]

Thomas and Jessie returned home before the Christmas of 1895, full of faith and threw themselves into the work of winning souls. Thomas Champness (1832-1905), who began *Joyful News* (1883-1955), thought it wise to put two vans on the road laden with books and the evangelists travelled through villages and market places selling books. Thomas Cook borrowed the idea from Champness and started a movement which is known as Gospel Mission Cars. Each evangelist sold his wares wherever he was and preaching wherever he could. In 1901 Thomas built five new vans at a cost of £750 and put them on the road. The fairs and markets had been visited all over the North of England, thousands of homes had been visited, evangelistic services had been held on a large scale and hundreds of sinners had been saved. When Thomas ceased to be a Connexional

---

[43] Thomas Cook, *Days of God's Right Hand*, pp.326, 327.

Evangelist, thirty of these cars were at work, in charge of thirty-six evangelists. In the year 1903-04 these lay evangelists conducted eight thousand, one hundred and two services, and the number of enquirers at these services were six thousand, eight hundred and eighty-one. The movement was probably at its zenith but in the coming years it dwindled away. The Gospel Car enterprise had its day and while the sun shone a good deal of hay was made.

The Southport Methodist Holiness Convention grew out of the providences of God and it owes its identity to the second evangelical awakening in Britain from 1859 onwards. There was a conspicuous renewal of interest in the doctrine and experience of scriptural holiness, and the origin of this movement in the United Kingdom can be traced to the holiness groups which began after the Civil War. Charles G. Finney, a leading figure in the Oberlin School of theology, had absorbed John Wesley's, *A Plain Account of Christian Perfection*, and adopted it with certain modifications. James Caughey (1810-1891), Irishman, was a Methodist and he strove also for the proclamation of holiness. Charles Palmer and his wife Phoebe were also Methodists and it was in their home that the famous 'Tuesday Meeting for the Promotion of Holiness' was held. The first general holiness meeting took place at Vineland, New Jersey, in 1867 and although it was interdenominational, attracted a number of Methodists. As a result of this gathering, the National Association for the Promotion of Holiness was formed. The Palmers, James Caughey, Daniel Steele, Bishop Matthew Simpson, John Inskip and J. A. Wood were to support the movement. Inskip and Wood came to England and preached the message of holiness in the full assurance of faith. Thomas Cook, still in his teens, travelled from his home in Middlesbrough to plead with them to come to the towns on the Tees and the Tyne.

As a result Cook later joined other lay evangelists in Methodism like Joshua Dawson, Robinson Watson and Jabez Wooley in urging believers to claim their inheritance in Christ by seeking victory over sin. In 1865 the Salvation Army, founded by William Booth, a convert under Caughey's ministry, set holiness at the centre of its witness. John G. Govan claimed the experience in 1884 and became the first instigator of the Faith Mission. Reader Harris began his work at Speke Hall in Battersea in 1885, leading eventually to the formation of the Pentecostal League of Prayer. Frank Crossley maintained a similar witness at the Star Hall in Manchester. In 1883 a Wesleyan Methodist minister, Thomas Champness, had published the first issue of *Joyful News*, and shortly afterwards began to train lay evangelists. Scriptural holiness was stressed from the start and the inheritance was later passed on to Cliff College through its first Principal, Thomas Cook, who was one of the pioneers of the Southport Convention.

Thomas Cook joined the Southport Convention in 1885 and while he did not start the Convention, his part in the proceedings was pivotal until his untimely death in 1912. He gave a message on perfect love and from a report in *The King's Highway*, there is every reason to believe that he was John Wesley's man. He maintained that every true Methodist believed the doctrine, and he expressed his opinion that no member could consistently remain in Methodist Society who spoke against this truth. He went on to define perfect love as pure love, that is, love without any opposition. Sin he declared was the opposite of love, and to be filled with love is to be emptied of sin. The two cannot exist together; perfect love is of the same kind as God's love. It is an impartation as well as a manifestation. This love is perfected to us, we love God because we cannot help it. This is the secret of true Christian liberty. Perfect love is perfect in quantity. We can only love God with the powers we possess; God requires nothing more. 'With all thy heart' is the commandment. Henry Smart gives this impression of Cook.

> This outline only gives an inadequate impression of the address, but it will be seen that the young evangelist spoke then with no uncertain sound on this wonderful Christian duty and privilege. He rightly divided the word of truth. Yet he was but twenty-six; he had received no theological training, nor was he a scholar, in the ordinary connotation of that term. Whence, then, had he the wisdom he displayed? He fed the people then and always with knowledge and

understanding, for he was a shepherd according to God's heart. His habits of prayer did for him what research does for the man of science – made him an expert in the things of God, even in his early manhood.... Later in the same week he gave another address, based on Romans 6:11. In this exposition of the doctrine he distinguished between sin as an act and sin as a state, and he insisted that we need to be saved not merely from acts of sin but from sin itself. He proceeded to draw a distinction between the conditional and absolute death of sin. To receive this blessing it was necessary to reckon ourselves dead unto sin; God would make the reckoning good, through our Lord Jesus Christ. 'I reckon myself dead unto sin now.' Who else will claim this freedom? Thank God, many do. Henceforth we live, but not we, Christ liveth in us (Gal. 2:20). [44]

At a meeting of Cliff College Committee, Henry Pope expressed the view that Thomas Cook's experience as a Connexional Evangelist had been a divine preparation for his appointment as Principal. Champness had launched the Joyful News Training Home and Mission, in his manse at Bolton and then at Castleton Hall, Rochdale. The aim of the College, as carrying on the tradition established in Lancashire, was to provide Methodist local preachers with a course in Bible knowledge and evangelistic methods. Then those trained at Cliff might either return to their circuit or in some cases be placed somewhere else on a full-time basis. There was a man qualified to take residence as a Principal and that man was Thomas Cook.

When Cook accepted Cliff College, it was good news to Thomas Champness and he wrote a letter to Thomas, full of gratitude and praise.

Will you allow me to say how thankful I am to God and to yourself for opening a way by which my wife and I can be relieved of the burden which had begun to press us down? Sometimes people have said to me, 'Champness, what is to become of your work when you are gone?' Providence incarnated in yourself has answered that question, and I have the joy of knowing that the work has now become a permanent factor in Methodism. With such a Staff and such a Head I do not see

---

[44] Henry Smart, *The Life of Thomas Cook, Evangelist*, pp.173, 174.

how Cliff College can be anything else but a helper of good things for the young preachers of Methodism.[45]

When Arthur Skevington Wood, the Principal of Cliff College, wrote, *On Fire For God: The Story of Thomas Cook,* he paid a tribute to the man and his work.

> Not only did Cook ensure that the evangelistic thrust of the new College should fulfil the original intention of the former Joyful News Training Home and Mission, but he also intensified the emphasis which Champness had placed on Scriptural holiness. Cook furthermore displayed gifts of administration in the management of the College with its expanding premises and adjoining farm to a degree that evidently opened the eyes even of some who knew him best. His tact and courtesy were unfailing. He revealed himself as a diplomat in pleading the cause of Cliff in the courts of the Church and quickly won the confidence both of the Conference and the Connexion. It was largely due to Cook's stature and skill that the transition from Rochdale to Calver was effected so smoothly. Within two years the Cliff building turned out to be too small for the numbers enrolling and the Champness Memorial Wing was added.[46]

Thomas Cook revelled in his work at Cliff College and his prayer, gospel preaching and the fact that he expected all Methodists to be full of the Spirit, was a joy to watch. When he was there two years, and the cost of the building and the repairs had been raised, he had so many applications from young men who wanted to come, he was led to the conclusion that he ought to add another wing to the building. The Committee counselled delay but admitted he could go ahead if he first secured the cost. In the following week he inserted a notice in *Joyful News* that he needed a thousand pounds and if anyone could manage this sum, he would go ahead. Next day he was going to Manchester and the lady he met there had often met his need in times of crises. The friend asked about Cliff College; was it full and had he any difficulty in getting students? He reported that it was full and he had to turn away eligible students. 'Then enlarge it,' was the advice of

---

[45]   Henry Smart, *The Life of Thomas Cook, Evangelist*, pp.192, 193.

[46]   A. Skevington Wood, *On Fire For God*, (1983), p.29.

the friend. 'Because I have not the money,' was his answer. Then his friend said, 'I have a thousand pounds of the Lord's money in the bank; I will give it to you.' Cook asked, 'Have you seen *Joyful News* this week?' The lady said she had not. Thomas Cook then told her of his appeal and she closed the incident by saying, 'I am glad to have a share in the work; this interview is evidently of God; I will send you a cheque for the amount in the morning.'[47]

In 1906 Thomas Cook built a new chapel in Eyam, famous for the great plague that had once raged there. The building is a pleasant one and its erection was a work of love to Thomas. Many of his friends supported him well and he was able to raise the money in due course. This fine building will be one of his memorials, just as the chapel at Lutterworth is one of Thomas Champness' memorials. Near to the finishing of the chapel, the telephone bell rang and it was the contractor wishing to have his money to date. Thomas didn't have it but he was sure that if the contractor could wait, it would be all right. Twenty minutes later and Thomas told him that he was sure that he would get more than he asked for. A week later he told that a man had sent him more than he desired and that the fifty pounds paid off the contractor.

Mrs. Cook, in her capacity as his help-meet, told often how prayer was with him a matter of routine.

> Prayer with him was always talking with God. He believed in closing the financial year at the college free from debt. One year there was a good deal wanted as the critical time approached, and he was obliged to go to Southport to take part in the Convention. He left instruction for his letters to be forwarded, and when at Southport he watched the post come and go. The last three days came, and he was short of a hundred pounds. He entered the tent at the usual time and before the service began prayed privately once more for what he needed. Looking up, he saw a lady beckoning to him, and when he went to her she said, 'Mr. Cook, the Lord told me to give you this this morning,' and she handed him a letter. He took the letter and put it in his pocket without opening it. When the service was over he opened it and found it

---

[47] Henry Smart, *The Life of Thomas Cook, Evangelist*, pp.216, 217.

contained a banknote for one hundred pounds for his work. The next day the same friend gave him a hundred pounds again, towards the debt on the tutor's house, then in course of liquidation.[48]

Nine years Thomas Cook was Principal of Cliff College and it was well known that the college was safe in the hands of one who would gather from all his significant sources. He only to had make his wants known and it seemed as if cheque books were placed at his disposal. They had a united view of his judgment and equally in his conscientious use of the money with which he was entrusted. During his Principalship not less than sixty thousand pounds have passed through his hands, and all accounts were audited every year by professional businessmen. Thomas acted on this principle and he could at any time submit his balance sheet to his Divine Employer, in the firm belief that he would be pronounced faithful in his unrighteous mammon as well as in his trust of the true riches. The utmost care was taken in the purchase of all commodities, and in the sale of the produce of the farm, and one had the greater pleasure in helping to support the enterprise because he knew perfectly well that every penny would be made to go as far as it possibly could. In this part of the work Thomas was greatly helped by his wife Jessie who controlled the domestic arrangements of the college with great ability, her bringing up as a farmer's daughter having prepared her for the position she so well filled.

Vallance Cook, younger brother of Thomas Cook, in his book, *Thomas Cook Evangelist-Saint*, wrote of how much his brother made up all the qualities he was expecting.

> This volume is a brother's tribute of love; a wreath placed upon the brow of one whom he regarded as the saintliest of men and the noblest of brothers. My brother lived a grand life and did a great work, but the greatest thing that has been said of him is that the love of God transfigured his countenance and irradiated his life. He was the most winsome of men, and all I have written is but to show how he lived the beautiful Gospel that he preached. And how he magnified the grace of God in all he spoke or wrote or did.... First, the fact that the

---

[48]   Henry Smart, *The Life of Thomas Cook, Evangelist*, pp.220, 221.

'Appreciation' has been made a blessing to thousands; and, secondly, because I am persuaded that no one can read of such a lovable and saintly man, as I know my brother to have been, without being moved to higher and better things. I pray God that it may be used for the furtherance of those aims and ideals that were the root of my brother's peace and joy, love and passion, and that gave such breadth and power to his evangel and his saintliness.[49]

Years afterwards, when about midway through his evangelistic career, Thomas conducted a mission at Hampstead, London, and Revd. T. E. Westerdale, Superintendent Minister, wrote of it as follows:

As long as I live, I shall never forget the scene of the last Sunday night. A mysterious, blessed, all-gracious power had been concentrating about the mission all the week through. At seven o'clock, when the service began, every seat was taken – gallery and downstairs, behind the pulpit, on the steps, in the communion rail. It was a glorious sight. It seemed all through the mission that he, Thomas Cook, was the very representative of the King. He stood like one anointed from the very presence of the Master.... I don't know what it was in the days of John Wesley or in the days of the early Methodist preachers. I used to witness some glorious scenes myself, twenty years ago, in the Melton Mowbray Circuit, when revival services were less scientific than they are now, but I have never witnessed a scene like Sunday night. The Lord is not dead yet. He is mighty to save. I have heard every sermon save one of this mission, and the sustaining power of each sermon has been marvellous. Mr. Cook is a great preacher; he lives possessed by the Master's spirit; but it is quite true that he is a man of extraordinary intellectual power, and I attribute the success of the mission, under God's blessing, to that one fact more than any other – the clear, vivid, logical, irresistible way in which he brought home the truth of God to the conscience of the sinner, and the inimitable pathos with which he gently led the troubled soul to the blood that cleanseth.[50]

Vallance Cook, who remembers the years growing up with Thomas and recalls the thirty years while they were both in the work, recalls:

---

[49] Vallance Cook, *Thomas Cook Evangelist-Saint*, (1931), Preface, pp.5, 6.
[50] Vallance Cook, *Thomas Cook Evangelist-Saint*, pp.59, 61.

My brother lived the life. It has been said that this is better than teaching or preaching the doctrine. Perhaps so; but it is still better when a man is able to do both. The teacher who translates his words into action is destined to accomplish far more than one who simply *does*, and yet can give no reasoned statement of the why and the wherefore, to say nothing of the man who teaches and yet does not follow his own precepts. Nothing is more powerful than theory backed up by practice. This is where he had the advantage, and why during the course of his ministry he led thousands into the light, and the *life*. His ideal was an attainable ideal, his saintliness a possible saintliness, and his holiness a practical holiness. He lived that which he taught.[51]

Nehemiah Curnock spent years admiring Thomas Cook, and he wrote of what he had found.

I seem to read Thomas Cook and all phases of his work like an open book. Everywhere throughout the years, and in every detail, great and small, of a winsome life, I cannot help seeing the good hand of God. He was, I think, the most godly man I ever knew. And the strangest thing of all was the utter naturalness of his godliness. You could not help falling in love with the man's religion. I have watched old men not far from the end of their pilgrimage, and young fellows fresh from school and college and city office, and young girls full of life and joy, all alike fall under the spell, not of his preaching, but of his personality. How they loved him, reverenced his masterful will, and secretly longed to be themselves more like him.[52]

Thomas wrote four books: *My Mission Tour in South Africa: A Record of Interesting Travel and Pentecostal Blessing* (1894); *Days Of God's Right Hand* (1896); *Soul-Saving Preaching* (1907); *New Testament Holiness* (1902), and various tracts; *First Steps in the Way of Life; Entire Cleansing; Scriptural Perfection*. There was one book he published in 1902, and its second and third editions came out in 1905 and 1909. The book was called *New Testament Holiness*, and today is available everywhere. Vallance Cook talks about it in glowing terms.

---

[51] Vallance Cook, *Thomas Cook Evangelist-Saint*, pp.110, 111.
[52] Vallance Cook, *Thomas Cook Evangelist-Saint*, p.138.

My brother's next book – which I do not hesitate to describe as his greatest and most important work, and from which many quotations are made in this volume – was entitled *New Testament Holiness*. It is, perhaps, the most clear, practical, and complete treatise on this great subject that has yet been printed in the English language. It has sold by the thousand, and hundreds have been led into the light through perusing its carefully-written pages. And as my object in writing this book is to present a picture of Thomas Cook as he really was in his inner and spiritual life, I here reproduce the account, as printed in *New Testament Holiness,* of his entrance into the blessing of full salvation.[53]

Arthur Skevington Wood, Principal of Cliff College, writes of the interest in Thomas's book.

The quintessence of Cook's teaching on this vital subject is contained in his best-known book entitled *New Testament Holiness*, which appeared in 1902 not long before he became Principal of Cliff College. It is right treasured still as a classic of its kind. Cook had sought to consider every aspect of his subject. He was steeped in the Scriptures which bore on it and each chapter is based on biblical revelation. He had thoroughly familiarized himself with what Wesley had written as contained in his collected Works. The view of other Methodist writers were known to him, in addition to those of the more recent American holiness school. His reading enriched and strengthened his original insights into the doctrine and experience of total sanctification but he saw no necessity for any drastic modification.[54]

Charles Wesley has brought sanctification into everyday living and there are plenty of hymns for which quotations are given. In 1767 there is found a hymn which clearly shows a second work of grace and people have sung it with experience.

>   Speak the second time, 'Be clean'
>   Take away my inbred sin
>   Every stumbling-block remove
>   Cast it out by perfect love.[55]

---

[53] Vallance Cook, *Thomas Cook Evangelist-Saint*, p.74.
[54] A. Skevington Wood, *On Fire For God*, p.27.
[55] Charles Wesley, *The Poetical Works*, Vol. 5, p.306, 'Jesu, cast a pitying eye.'

Henry Smart, in his book, *The Life of Thomas Cook, Evangelist*, uses it to prove that Thomas Cook was attracted by that hymn and certainly used it.

> This was the doctrine Thomas Cook preached, and which it pleased God signally to bless when His servant bore witness to it. No man in the Wesleyan ministry during the last thirty years has made that truth such a conspicuous part of his preaching as brother Cook did. It was essentially part of *his* gospel, and perhaps the most prominent part also. His correspondence shows what a great hunger there was for this blessing, and also the infinite difference it made when believers were fully sanctified and 'favoured with God's peculiar smile,' and 'with every blessing blessed.'[56]

Writing on, *Thomas Cook Evangelist*, in 2007, Robert Evans says it was a natural part of a preacher who clearly made John Wesley theology the passion of his life.

> A natural corollary of the New Birth is John Wesley's doctrine of Christian Perfection. Wesley taught that if a person is completely trusting in the cleansing power of Christ, and lived close to Him, then it is possible to live without committing any sins that we were aware of.... Over the years following Wesley's death, other terms came to be used for this doctrine which did not carry misleading inferences and meanings flowing from the name to the same degree. Saintly people like John Hunt called it 'Entire Sanctification.' Others called it 'Perfect Love.' Thomas Cook was one of these. He also called it 'Scriptural Holiness,' or 'New Testament Holiness.' It was this last title which he used for his book, in order to emphasise that whatever peculiar features, in the eyes of some, the teaching might have, it was simple Bible teaching, and that was its main quality.[57]

In the *Preface* to the book, Thomas tells the story of one Theological Institution where the students asked the tutor to give a definition of holiness. The tutor expressed the opinion that it was 'an eternal approximation towards an unrealisable ideal', but added that an Evangelist emphasised the definite view of holiness which Mr. Wesley taught and he was loath to speak against it. Thomas referred

---

[56] Henry Smart, *The Life of Thomas Cook, Evangelist*, pp.277, 278
[57] Robert Evans, *Thomas Cook Evangelist*, (2007), pp.20, 21.

to himself, that he was the evangelist, and that this book would be an exposition of this doctrine. 'It contains the substance of the addresses which were so much blessed to the congregation mentioned, and which have been used of God to help Christian people into the higher Christian life in many parts of the world.'[58] The book is divided into twenty-five chapters and it has roughly eight pages per chapter. It is one of the books that has been printed many times and in all the literature of holiness, this is one of the best. There are quotations from much reading but they are not marked nor is any literature quoted. They are proof that Thomas has read fairly widely and the book abounds with quotations. Samuel Rutherford, John Bunyan, John and Charles Wesley, John Fletcher, Adam Clarke, Richard Watson, William Pope, Daniel Steele, Henry Drummond, William and Catherine Booth, Dwight Moody, Robert Murray M'Cheyne, Thomas Collins, Alexander Maclaren, Asa Mahan and dozens more.

In the opening chapter, he deals with 'Blameless, not Faultless'. In the Bible the word is rendered 'blameless;' see I Cor. 1; 8; Phil. 2:15; 1 Thess. 5:23, 1 Tim. 5:7. Scripture doesn't make 'faultless', a sign of purity but it makes 'blameless' the mark of those who are sanctified.

> Grace does not make men infallible. Sin has so perverted our moral and spiritual powers, that we shall never in this present life be free from infirmities of human nature. Whatever our experience of the grace of God may be, the liability to error will cling to us until this mortal puts on immortality. Infirmities have their ground in our physical nature, aggravated by intellectual deficiencies. They are the outflow of our imperfect moral organisation – the scars of sin which remain after the wound has been healed. A cut limb may be cured, but the scar remains for ever.... Then, when death has reduced us to dust, and the Divine Potter has re-made us, body as well as soul, we shall be 'presented faultless before the presence of His glory with exceeding joy' (Jude 24), but 'until the coming of our Lord Jesus Christ' (1 Thess. 3:13), all we can hope for is to be preserved *without blame*.[59]

---

58 Thomas Cook, *New Testament Holiness*, Preface, p.4.
59 Thomas Cook, *New Testament Holiness*, pp.11, 12.

In Chapter 3 Cook deals with the fact that 'Sin Not a Necessity', and should not be found in the Christian life. Holiness secures the safest possible condition on earth, but absolute security does not belong in this present world. People assert that the doctrine of entire extirpation of sin from the heart puts the soul beyond real temptation, but this is a fallacy and the assumption is much too broad. It renders angels in probation, Adam in Eden, and our Lord Himself, incapable of real temptation. However the fact that some angels fell, that Adam sinned, and that Jesus Christ 'was in all points tempted as we are' (Heb. 4:15), should be sufficient proof that holy souls are capable of temptation. If angels and Adam fell we shall need to watch and pray and keep our hearts with all diligence. We shall pray and keep watch and be on our guard lest we become 'entangled again in the yoke of bondage.' Eternal vigilance is the price of safety and grace never induces presumption. Let all those be warned: 'Let him that thinks he stands take heed lest he fall' (1 Cor. 10:12).

The New Testament teaches that the salvation which Jesus provides includes grace to live without sinning. Paul puts a question before declaring that probation is essential. 'Shall we continue in sin that grace may abound? God forbid. How shall we that are dead to sin live any longer therein' (Rom. 6:1, 2)? In writing to the Thessalonians he says, 'You are witnesses and God also how, how holy and righteous and blameless was our behaviour to you believers' (I Thess. 2:10). These were strong words for a man to use but they were true. The life he lived was declared to be by the Holy Spirit holy and just and unblameable. John's teaching exactly coincides with that of Paul and the purposes of his epistles was to warn believers against sin and to keep them from it. 'These things I am writing to you that you may not sin,' (I John 2:1).

> The scriptural doctrine is undoubtedly this: Christians need not, and do not sin, but capability to sin remains. Should one be overtaken in a fault let him not despair. God, in His mercy, has made sufficient provision in Christ for his forgiveness and cleansing again, if he confesses the wrong he has done. Much controversy about sin results from the want of accuracy in the definition of the term. We do not in this chapter understand by sin involuntary deviation from the known law of God.

44

What is commonly meant by *committing sin*, in the New Testament, is a willing and known transgression of a known law.... Sins demand a personal confession and personal resort to the blood of sprinkling, and an act of reliance upon Christ; but involuntary transgressions, so called sins of ignorance, are covered by the blood of Christ without any definite act of faith on the part of the believer. Evils arising out of unavoidable ignorance are certainly not sins in the sense of attaching guilt to the perpetrator. They are his misfortune, not his fault. Their penalty may be suffering, but it is not condemnation. If it were condemnation, we should always be in bondage, because we come short of God's absolute standard of right every moment of our lives.[60]

In Chapter 5 Thomas deals with 'The New Birth and Entire Sanctification'. Perhaps a person exulting in the new birth may feel that all sin is gone and rejoices that in regenerated he is set apart for God. He is made a new creature in Christ Jesus and new and heavenly life is breathed into him by the Holy Spirit. He is translated out of darkness into marvellous light. The dominion of sin is broken and the love of God is shed abroad in his heart. His desires, tastes, impulses, aims, and aspirations are all changed. Regeneration is holiness begun, but before too long sin is suspended but not destroyed. The disease is modified but not eradicated. The bitter and baneful thing is nipped in the bud, some of the branches are lopped off but the root is not removed. Tendencies to sin are controlled but they are not extirpated. There is still a warfare within, a sort of duality, in which flesh and spirit antagonise each other. It is a state of mixedness in which Christians in a degree, according to the measure of their faith, are spiritual, yet in a degree they are carnal.

> Regeneration is the beginning of purification. Entire sanctification is the finishing of that work. Entire sanctification removes from the soul all the elements which antagonise the element of holiness planted in regeneration. It is an elimination, as dross is separated from the gold by fire. It is an eradication, the removal of all roots of bitterness, the seeds of sin's disease. It is a crucifixion, the putting to death of the body or the life of sin. It is such a complete renewal of the heart that

---

[60] Thomas Cook, *New Testament Holiness*, pp.22, 23.

sin has no longer any place within, its last remains are scattered, the war within the citadel ceases and God reigns without a rival.[61]

In Chapter 10 Thomas deals with 'Evangelical Perfection', and the words 'holiness', 'perfect love', and 'perfection', are used interchangeably. Perfect love is expressive of the spirit and temper, the moral atmosphere in which the entirely sanctified Christian lives. The word 'perfection' signifies that spiritual completeness or wholeness into which the soul enters when the last inward foe is conquered and the last distracting force harmonised with the mighty love of Christ and every energy employed in the delightful service of a wonderful Saviour. As Cook explains:

> No word has been the occasion of so much stumbling and controversy among Christians as this word 'perfect.' But the term is a Scriptural one, and is used more frequently in the Bible that any other single term to set forth Christian experience. It occurs one hundred and thirty-eight times in the Scriptures, and in more than fifty of these instances it refers to human character under the operations of grace. Early in Divine revelation, we find Jehovah saying to Abraham, 'Walk before Me and be perfect,' (Gen. 17:1), and to Moses, 'Thou shalt be perfect with the Lord.' (Deut. 18:13). Forty-five times the Israelites are commanded to bring sacrifices without blemish, and every time the word should have been perfect.... Opening the New Testament, we find the word 'perfect' dropping from the lips of Christ, and from the pen of St. Paul, seventeen times as descriptive of fitness for the kingdom of God; while the cognate noun *perfection* is twice used, and the verb *to perfect* fourteen times. Instead of finding fault with a word which the Spirit of inspiration sees fit to use with such persistence from the book of Genesis to the Epistles of St. John, should we not rather endeavour to arrive at its true Scriptural meaning?[62]

Let no person stagger at this immediateness. God always gives power to comply with His requirement, and duties are privileges while all commands are equivalent to promises. We can be sure that the command to love God now with a perfect love implies that He will give us power to do what He requires us to do. To maintain otherwise

---

61   Thomas Cook, *New Testament Holiness*, p.35.
62   Thomas Cook, *New Testament Holiness*, pp.66, 67.

is to charge God with mocking us with a command we are utterly unable to perform. What God requires *now* must be possible *now*; and if we will but claim as a present privilege what He reveals as a present duty, we shall immediately prove that 'the word is very nigh unto you, in your mouth, and in your heart, that you may do it' (Deut. 30:14).

In Chapter 11 Thomas Cook deals with 'The Fullness of the Spirit', and the conclusion is that the fullness is a synonym for entire sanctification. All inward renewal is the result of the Holy Spirit's operations and He is the indispensable agent in the production of spiritual life. Before Pentecost the Holy Spirit had been given to the disciples. Christ had breathed upon them and said, 'Receive the Holy Spirit' (John 20:22), but Pentecost made an unspeakable difference to them. The visible tongues of fire were only emblems of what had passed within. Their intellects were flooded with Divine light, their souls throbbed with Divine sympathies, and their tongues spoke so wonderfully of the things of God, that all who knew them were amazed, saying, 'What does this mean?' (Acts 2:12). They met together as the sincere but timid and partially enlightened followers of Christ, but they left the upper room full of light and power and love. They were now filled with the Holy Ghost as an all-illuminating, all-strengthening, all-sanctifying presence. The baptism of fire has consumed their inward depravity, subsidised all their faculties, and filled to the full each capacity with Divine energy and life. Thomas says:

> 'Baptised with' and 'filled with the Holy Spirit' are often convertible terms in the Acts of the Apostles, but it is instructive to note that they are not always so. The apostles received but one baptism, but they were 'filled' with the Spirit over and over again. The baptism of the Holy Ghost was, and still is, a sort of initiatory rite to the life of Pentecostal service, and fullness and victory. Christian life begins at Calvary, but effective service begins at Pentecost. Before Pentecost there was not much service rendered by the apostles that was worth the name. But with the Spirit's baptism they entered upon a new phase of life and service.... Almost all prominent Christian workers whose labours have been pre-eminently owned of God, bear witness to the

47

reception of a distinct definite blessing which they received subsequent to conversion, and which inaugurated a new era in their spiritual life. They had received their Pentecost, and the Holy Spirit was in them the fire of love, the light of assurance and the unction of power.[63]

In Chapter 23 Cook sets out five things that must be present in the Christian life, under the heading, 'How to Retain the Blessing'. From beginning to end in the work of salvation there must be both Divine and human action. If we are to be preserved we must persevere. It is true that salvation in one sense is all of God, but it is also true that the gifts and graces of the spirit are ours only when certain conditions are complied with. We are to 'work out' the salvation which God works within. To grow in grace we must avail ourselves of the means of grace. We are to keep ourselves in the love of God. This is true of entire sanctification as it is of any other state of grace.

1. **We Must Walk in The Light**. Consecration must keep pace with the ever-widening circle of illumination. As we rise higher in Christian life we shall have a clearer vision, quickened sensibilities, and increasing clear perception of what the will of God is. There is safety in no other course. The obedience of those who walk with God will often be tested by new revelations of His will.

> When they left the narrow track of implicit obedience to the leading of the Spirit, fellowship with God ceased, and the sense of the abiding of the Comforter was gone. Since then a shadow has been over their lives, they have made no progress, and have lacked both power and joy. Nor will they ever find the blessing again until they go back to the place where they dropped the thread of obedience, and perform the thing which God then demanded. From beginning to end, the Bible rings out with one long demand for uncompromising obedience.[64]

2. **We Must Keep a Life of Simple Trust**. The Christian must believe moment by moment that the blood of Jesus Christ cleanseth from all sin. On the first approach of temptation, doubt, or perplexity, it is time for the Christian to declare in their hearts that in spite of all

---

[63] Thomas Cook, *New Testament Holiness*, pp.76, 77.
[64] Thomas Cook, *New Testament Holiness*, p.158.

doubt, reason or sense, that the blood of Jesus does now cleanse from all sin. We must hold on by simple faith, insisting that God is true, until the trial is over. The Holy Spirit is an abiding guest in the heart of every sanctified Christian, but times will come when the sense of His Presence will be dulled.

> No greater mistake can be made than to measure our piety by our emotions. Our feelings are changeable as the wind and the tides, and fickle as April weather. Health, education, natural temperament, and much also apart from religion, combine to modify them. We must cease to consider how we feel, and build upon the immovable Rock of God's Word and faithfulness. We may tremble, but the Rock of Ages never does. None of our changeable moods can affect or alter the fact that the blood of Jesus cleanses from all sin. We must meet every suggestion of doubt by the decisive answer that God is faithful and must do as He has said.[65]

3. **We Must Take Time for Prayerful Meditation of the Word of God**. Christians should take time to read, mark and inwardly digest spiritual truth as they take time to grow and strengthen all the elements of spiritual life. The best devotional literature is only truly helpful so far as it has its roots in the true sayings of God. Hasty snatches of this Heavenly manna are not without benefit, but if we would dwell on high places we must make the Bible our chief Book. It is astonishing what new beauties are unfolded, what new wonders are discovered, what strength and comfort are derived, when we obey the command to Ezekiel, 'Son of Man, eat the roll' (Ezek.3:1).

4. **We Must Engage Actively in Christian Work**. The reflex influence of Christian work upon a man himself is scarcely less important and valuable than the direst influence upon unsaved souls. In it lies the secret of growth and joy. We can only save ourselves by trying to save others. We see with clearer eyes in trying to make others see. God's law is *use* or *lose*. In sending us to work God not only has the salvation of the lost at heart, but the best good of the Christian. Our duties are our wings. When we first assume them they seem like burdens, but cheerfully borne they become less and less

---

[65] Thomas Cook, *New Testament Holiness*, pp.158, 160.

heavy, and eventually become the wings by which we mount higher and higher into the life of God.

5. **We Must Never be Satisfied with Present Attainments**. Purity of heart is but the preparation for advancement in knowledge, love and holiness. There is no finality in this life of faith and charity. There are ever deeper depths to be fathomed and higher heights to be climbed. It is always from grace to grace, from strength to strength and from glory to glory. Growth is the great law of life in the spiritual as in the animal and vegetable kingdoms. By various figures and illustrations the Gospel represents growth as the Christian's privilege and duty. Now we have the leaven that works until the whole lump is leavened.

> Holiness deals with the inner condition, it fills the soul with love, joy and peace. The result is right conduct, and right conduct has permanent effects upon the character. It is not enough that 'we stand fast in the liberty wherewith God has made us free.' If we would grow in grace we must be always aiming at something above and beyond us. The last word is never said, the last effort is never made; to retain entire sanctification we must be ever 'reaching forth unto those things which are before.' We shall lose the grace we have unless we seek for more.[66]

Thomas Cook finished the book but he never knew the book would sell and sell. Three editions were sold during his life and at least fifteen were sold in the coming years. Thomas aimed for simplicity and candour and there are not many whose publications have run to fifteen editions. It is one of the small number that is sold and resold and that is what Cook wished for. The one hundred and seventy-eight pages are full of illustrations of how people sought the second blessing and retained it throughout their lives. The final nine pages are complete with Thomas Cook telling us his Testimony of how the Lord blessed him and used him after he sought and found the second blessing.

> How I wish I could tell of the sweetness, the richness, and indescribable blessedness of this life of perfect love. I cannot tell the story, but cannot let it alone. O, for a thousand tongues to proclaim

---

[66] Thomas Cook, *New Testament Holiness*, pp.163, 164.

Jesus to men, the mighty Saviour, who is able to save them to the uttermost who come unto God by Him! Reader, will you join us and help us to spread the sacred flame?[67]

After serving as a Lay Evangelist and Connexional Evangelist and during his nine years as Principal of Cliff College, he put into practice what he had written about in his book, *Soul-Saving Preaching,* written in 1906. With thirteen chapters on the art of preaching for a verdict, he writes about preaching and power. In chapter one, 'The Evangelistic Gift', he deals with some measure of the work into which they are called.

> Our theory of spiritual dynamics is this: The Holy Ghost sheds love abroad in the believer's heart, and love is power. This power is always effective to conquer sin and in its highest degree to overcome sin.... Causes produce effects; means conduce to ends. Soul-saving is not a mechanical process, but there are helps and there are hindrances. To win men for Christ there is required, in addition to personal consecration, tact, adaptation, knowledge of human nature, a forcible and direct manner of appeal, and much else that is human.... Dr. Alexander Whyte has told us how he made a patient and laborious study of John Wesley's *Journals* for the purpose of classifying all the texts upon which that great preacher built his evangel. We can learn much from studying the ways and means of those who have been instrumental in winning multitudes for the Lord.[68]

In chapter two, 'Definiteness of Aim', Cook holds firm his suggestion might have directions and purposes about souls needing to be one. Writing to his preachers about talents, Wesley counselled that it was not their business to preach so many sermons, but to save as many souls as possible and to lead them into that holiness without which no man can see the Lord. Adam Clarke's, *Letter to a Preacher*, said it was not merely to explain God's Word, but to save souls.[69] Whenever a preacher forgets this, he will go astray. A sermon is a speech having a definite aim, a result in the convictions, affections, resolutions and

---

[67] Thomas Cook, *New Testament Holiness*, p.178.
[68] Thomas Cook, *Soul-Saving Preaching*, (1906), pp.1, 12.
[69] Adam Clarke, *A Letter To A Preacher*, (1868), pp.8, 9.

conduct of the hearer. Preachers are effective, other things being equal, in proportion to the clearness of their purpose, and the definiteness of their aim. This aim at direct results is the secret of one half the success of Methodism. The careful study of the preachers who have wielded most power shows that they were actuated and thrilled by this great purpose, and that this made ordinary talents extraordinary and converted weakness into strength. Men who decide to live for this must be prepared to sacrifice everything that would interfere with the accomplishment of their purpose. They must prepare their sermons with the needs of the people in mind, and be willing to sacrifice personal tastes, literary ambitions, favourite lines of study, and make themselves of no reputation that by 'all means they might save some.' The people must leave our services saying not, 'What a preacher,' but, 'What a Saviour!'[70] Sin was never more aggressive. It has boldness, skill, and resources such as it never had before. Soul-saving means labour of body and brain, such as only men who are possessed by an all-engrossing purpose will attempt.

In the third chapter on his book Cook deals with 'What to Preach.' The Word of God is the chosen instrument of the Holy Spirit in the great work of soul-saving, especially the great truths of that Word which circle round the crucified and risen Lord. The subject-matter of Paul's preaching was Christ crucified. The very heart and essence of Peter's preaching is found in the words, 'Whom ye crucified, whom God raised from the dead' (Acts 2:23, 24). This was the central theme of all true preaching, the truth around which crystallizes the science of salvation. Much of the present-day preaching fails to reach, touch, and move men because the fact is not recognised that the Cross is the medicine of God for all the wants and woes of men, and the very heart of the Gospel is the substitutionary sacrifice. Preachers need to preach substitution straightforwardly and unmistakably, if the preacher longs to convert sinners and lead through repentance and faith to holiness. To this all other means and methods must be tributary and subsidiary. Thomas goes on:

---

[70] Thomas Cook, *Soul-Saving Preaching*, p.19.

Our business is to obey the Divine injunction. 'Show My people their transgression, and the house of Jacob their sins' (Isaiah 58:1) There is danger in these days of toning down the meaning of the word until it means something less altogether than what the Bible teaches, and what God means by sin. Some regard it as a sort of pardonable naughtiness for which men are to be pitied rather than blamed, the result of weakness rather than wickedness, but the Bible teaching is very different. Sin is lawlessness. It is setting up our will against God's will. Sin defies law because it is law; resists restraint because it is restraint; contests authority with God because He is God. That is the spirit of sin. It is rebellion against God. It sets Him at defiance, spurns His authority, and treats His government with contempt. Sin and salvation should always be proclaimed in one and the same breath. Christ must be set forth as able and willing to save to the uttermost. If we preach a present free and full salvation, sin-stricken hearts will be inspired with hope and gladness, and be led into the joy of conscious salvation.[71]

Thomas Cook makes 'Simple and Interesting' the next phase of his book. Hundreds of good men are failing in the pulpit today because they weight their sermons with technical and abstract terms which the people do not understand. It is a matter for serious consideration how much of what is said in the pulpit is really understood by the people. Let those who imagine that deep thought and big words must go together read the first chapter of St. John's Gospel. No profounder piece of composition was ever written, and most of it is in monosyllables. Learning is good so far as it helps us to communicate thought and feeling, but it becomes a peril and a snare if it produces a form of speech which is not understood by the common people. Even the educated people enjoy an earnest extempore delivery, and prefer sermons that abound in words which the heart knows to those full of high-sounding phrases and technical expressions. If we would win for the truth an entrance to the hearts of the people, we must learn to be familiar and natural, and to be free as the occasion may require. The head, the heart, and the imagination must all be appealed to. Mankind is possessed by a three-fold nature; reason, affection, and imagination. By awakening and gratifying the imagination the truth

---

[71] Thomas Cook, *Soul-Saving Preaching*, pp.27, 28.

finds its way more readily to the heart and makes a deeper impression on the memory.

While similes, metaphors, allegories and anecdotes are excellent and indispensable to successful preaching, the preacher is warned not to overwhelm the truth by excessive use of illustration. Real instruction must be given and solid doctrine taught, or else the preacher will fail. An illustration is but a window, but what use is the light which it admits if you have nothing for the light to reveal? The best illustrations are drawn from familiar life, and especially from personal experience. How often, when the rest of the discourse has apparently failed to impress, have the people melted with emotion as the preacher has told the simple story of conversion. Such references never failed to kindle their own religious feelings and to embrace a sympathetic emotion through their congregations. The preacher cannot improve upon this mode of illustrating the truths he is sent to proclaim.

Thomas then deals with 'Earnestness', and he lays down a statement which Dr. Campbell Morgan pressed home at a Southport Convention. 'Indifference in the world is largely the result of passionlessness in the pulpit.'[72]

There is an undercurrent of suspicion abroad that much of the preaching of today is but make-believe, and that suspicion is due to the formal, lifeless manner in which the duties of the preacher are too often performed. How can a man really believe in the great, solemn, eternal verities that he preaches without being thrilled with intense emotion to the very core of his being? Who can tell how much such a reflection as this has to do with the prevailing alienation of so many of the people from our Churches? To the man who believes that God has called him to be His spokesman – to publish the command on which hangs the eternal destiny of those who are reached by the sound of his voice – how is it possible to preach with unquivering nerve and unquickened heart-beat? His soul should glow and quiver under the

---

[72] Thomas Cook, *Soul-Saving Preaching*, p.51.

tremendous burden of his message, until, like an irrepressible fire or flood, it must have vent somewhere.[73]

The history of preaching is trumpet-tongued in proclaiming passion as the quality most essential to success. In all ages the successful preachers have been made men whose souls were moved with a sense of the tremendous import of their commission, and their burning hearts soon found for themselves flaming tongues which passionately proclaimed the claims of God upon the human race. The passion and fervour of the preachers on the Day of Pentecost has passed into a proverb. The passion of Paul throbs and burns in every chapter of his marvellous career. There is no true earnestness apart from a right view of the Cross, a realisation of things unseen, and the preacher's responsibilities. Such are the men God uses; men whose souls throb with Divine sympathies, and who say, as Paul says, 'This one thing I do' (Phil. 3:13).

In chapter eight of his book, Thomas deals with 'Application', and begins with two extracts from the *Journal* of John Wesley. What Wesley thought about preaching without application is seen in two quotations. Wesley visited Glasgow in 1774 and he thought himself fortunate in hearing two the sermons. 'My spirit was moved within me at the sermons I heard both morning and afternoon. They contained much truth, but were no more to awaken one soul than an Italian opera.'[74] The other sermon he heard was in Aberdeen in 1779 when he recorded: 'This very day I heard many excellent truths at the Kirk, but as there was no application it was likely to do as much good as the singing of a lark.'[75] Preaching, when it is endowed with Divine power, is the spreading of God's truth over the whole man until it touches intellect, sensibilities, affections, and will, but it should appeal especially to the conscience. This was the effect of our Lord's ministry; some were saved and others 'walked no more with Him,' (John 6:66). It is better to offend men and women than harden them

---

[73] Thomas Cook, *Soul-Saving Preaching*, pp.51, 52.
[74] John Wesley, *Journal*, (1909), Vol. 6, p.19.
[75] John Wesley, *Journal*, Vol. 6, p.239.

in sin, and nothing is so hardening as the Gospel if it is not responded to. Preachers should make Felix tremble, Herod acknowledge that God is with us, and make David feel that he is the man; then we must study the necessities of the people, find out their errors and sins and false refuges, and what are the truths they most need. Our business is to probe the wound and touch the very quick of the soul. Only by this means will sinners be pricked in their hearts and we must labour to remove prejudices, to resolve doubts, to conquer objections, and to drive the sinner out of their hiding place.

Familiarity with truths takes away their force and blunts their edge and for this reason we need to emphasise admitted truths by varied and repeated re-statement. To our unconverted hearers, only those sermons are worth anything which single out each person, saying, 'Thou are the man'. As Thomas puts it:

> All successful soul-winners have cultivated this directness of appeal. It is this sort of preaching, searching the inmost recesses of the soul, dragging forth to the view of conscience the innumerable sins that are hidden under the successive layers of deep and thick darkness, which lead men to cry, 'Sirs, what must I do to be saved?' (Acts 16:30). The preaching a worlding likes is that which will permit him to keep on living in sin and yet feel fairly comfortable.... For this reason we need frequently to emphasise admitted truths by varied and repeated restatement.... Preachers should never forget that preaching is destined for immediate effect. We always miss the mark when we preach with the idea of doing good at some other time. Present impression must be our constant aim. 'Now is the accepted time; now is the day of salvation' (2 Cor. 6:2). Our sermon may be the last which some poor sinner may hear before he is summoned to the bar of God. There is something awfully solemn in the thought that while we are preaching, some hearer's probation may end and his salvation or damnation begin. 'Who is sufficient for these things?' (2 Cor. 2:16).)[76]

Thomas Cook then deals with 'Pulling in the Net', as he contemplates the preacher dealing with those who have shown an interest. The After-meeting is about catching men and women for God and where

---

[76] Thomas Cook, *Soul-Saving Preaching*, pp.60-63.

it is not used, the preacher has lost many of the people. Preaching deals with men and women in the mass but they are converted one by one. With few exceptions, the Word of God must be followed by personal dealing and the After-meeting meets this demand. Where it is used wisely and properly, this service brings anxious seekers in to contact with ministers and other workers and it gives good instructions at the critical state of their religious history. Cook then gives instruction on how the After-meeting should be employed.

> Preachers vary much in their methods of conducting these meetings, but all agree that to be successful there must be as little break as possible between the preaching service and the meeting which follows. The one should merge into the other without interruptions, diversion or delay. Even a slight diversion may drive away all real concern and dissipate impressions. Anthems, vespers, and organ postludes sometimes destroy the continuity which is essential to success.... Let it be remembered that the man who has preached has more influence with the congregation while his spell is upon them than any other person is likely to have. For this reason it is often best for the preacher to conduct the After-meeting single-handed, to plead with God and the people alternately, and not to allow any but himself to lead in audible prayer. This method does more than maintain continuity; it prevents those persons inflicting themselves upon the meeting whose dreary repetitions have become intolerable to all except those who are seasoned.[77]

Thomas Cook reserves his last chapter but one to 'Pentecostal Power', and he has much to say on this topic. No one was ever saved merely by preaching the Gospel. It is the Gospel applied and enforced by the Holy Spirit that saves men and women. Clear views of truth may be set forth but without the Spirit's anointing no convincing power will attend their enunciation. All natural gifts are good but they are perilous if depended upon instead of the Holy Spirit. Cook alludes to his 'Pentecostal Power' by drawing attention to its absence.

> It is lamentable to see how frequently preachers take that one and essential condition of success – the presence and power of the Holy Spirit – for granted, while they spare no pains to secure all other

---

[77] Thomas Cook, *Soul-Saving Preaching*, pp.76, 77.

elements of necessary preparation. No preacher can be inspired to the maximum of possible service who has not received the baptism of the Holy Spirit. It was this Pentecostal baptism that prepared the Apostles for their work. Before Pentecost there was not much service rendered by them that was worth the name, but with the Spirit's baptism they entered upon a new phase of life and service. The visible tongues of fire were only emblems of what had passed within. What new creatures they then became! They were raised to a new altitude; a new energy and force possessed them. With this experience difficulties melted into empty air. There was no limit to their hopes, because there was no limit to their power. Nothing could resist the wisdom and Spirit by which they spoke. Within one generation Paganism was shaken to the centre, and Christianity had spread throughout the known world.[78]

The baptism of the Holy Spirit was and still is, the initiatory rite to the life of Pentecostal service and victory. No one can read the lives of the early Methodist preachers without being impressed with the fact that those whose labours were pre-eminently owned by God bear witness to the reception of a distinct definite blessing which they received subsequent to conversion. Some of them termed it 'the second blessing', but they really received their Pentecost, and suddenly became bold, mighty, aggressive and conquering. Speaking to an almost exclusive Methodist audience in Cliff College, Thomas felt there was no place like it for urging the Methodist doctrine of second blessing holiness.

Have we not known men who possessed this wonderful gift? They seemed to be able to look into the very souls of their hearers, and to talk to them with an almost Divine authority and instantaneous effect. Some of them were not profound thinkers, or powerful speakers, but they were wholly devoted to God and full of desire for the salvation of souls. When they spoke they seemed surcharged with an energy which could not be called their own. They had a something which touches the tongue and enables them to declare with astonishing effectiveness the message of grace.... They had received that Divine enduement which is called *unction* - the crowning gift of the Holy Spirit for service. It is neither pathos, nor eloquence, nor psychological power, nor mental force; but a subtle, mysterious, unaccountable, and almost irresistible

---

[78] Thomas Cook, *Soul-Saving Preaching*, pp.87-89.

influence which God alone can bestow. No words can describe the gift, but it may be known and felt by all.[79]

Thomas Cook knew that Cliff College, opened for the betterment of Methodist preachers, would take all this, and it is no surprise that this doctrine was gladly received. Cook knew that there were men thirsting for this blessing and he closed on a populist note.

> We know nothing else that is needed to make many preachers all that God meant them to be, but this baptism of fire. Nothing burns its way through all obstacles like fire. Nothing can stand before it. Give us men on fire with the Holy Spirit, and nothing can prevent Christianity from becoming the all-conquering power in the world as it is destined to be. The wonder is that any preacher can be content to work without this priceless gift. Much better would it be for the world if the Church would cease making weak efforts to save it, and wait upon God until it is endued with this power from on high. With it we shall accomplish more in one year than in a hundred years of working in our own strength. We claim to be sharers of Pentecostal privileges, and yet how few have received this baptism which Christ is exalted to bestow.[80]

Thomas Cook said in his *Preface* that this book contains 'three or four addresses given at different times to Cliff College Students on the subject of Soul-Saving Preaching.... The future of Methodism must depend more and more on the efficiency of those who fill the pulpit, and.... five out of every seven of our pulpits are supplied by local preachers every Sunday....'[81] There are ninety-two pages covering thirteen chapters, and Thomas Cook drives it home that only preachers filled with the Holy Spirit can minister these things. No matter what a preacher may claim and tries to prove it, nothing can succeed like a preacher filled with the Spirit and on fire with God. As the *Preface* makes out, Thomas meant that his book would be used time and again on students and with the earnest prayer on being filled and filled again by the Holy Spirit. During his thirty-four years in Methodism, his plea always was - get the people converted and then

---

[79] Thomas Cook, *Soul-Saving Preaching*, pp.89, 90.
[80] Thomas Cook, *Soul-Saving Preaching*, pp.91, 92.
[81] Thomas Cook, *Soul-Saving Preaching*, Preface.

get them filled with the Holy Ghost and fire. In all his preaching, at home, in Ireland, in South Africa, in Australia, in New Zealand and in Sri Lanka, his plea was always this; men and women are perishing in their sin and Jesus has died and rose again to bring to sinners everlasting life. He was a Methodist through and through and all his life he revelled in Methodist doctrine.

Thomas Cook met and came to know Frank and Emily Crossley who lived at Bowden, Manchester, and with his brother William, ran the Crossley's Gas Engine at their works at Openshaw. Thomas met Frank on many occasions and they struck up a friendship which lasted until Frank died early in March 1897. Frank gave away millions of pounds and later he believed God was calling him to the Salvation Army. Instead God wanted him to work in Manchester and he moved with his family and bought Star Hall in Manchester. His daughter, Ella Crossley, tells the story of how her father turned round the fortunes of two brothers.

> I was returning from London to Harrogate late one night and found I had an hour to wait at Leeds station, so I went into the waiting room intending to spend the time there. When I entered, I saw a man standing near to the fire with his arm leaning on the mantel. His eyes looked as though he had been weeping, so I asked him if he were in trouble. When he heard my voice he looked up with a start and said, 'Is that you Mr. Cook?' and told me he had heard me preach several times in the chapel that he attended. When I asked him what was the cause of his sorrow, his only reply was, 'I have met a man today who has treated me like Jesus Christ would have done.' I asked for particulars and he told me something as follows:
>
> Two or three years ago my brother and I decided to start business on our own account. We purchased a factory and brought one of Crossley's gas engines to supply the power. After we got the engine fixed we found we had not purchased one large enough to do the amount of work to make the business pay, and instead of making money by our venture we lost it. Things got worse and worse with us until a few weeks ago my brother said, 'It is no use carrying on any longer, we are bankrupt.' He urged that we should sign our petition at once and get matters settled, but I said, 'Think what a disgrace it will be. We are both of us church members and Sunday-school teachers,

and I cannot bear the thought of bringing discredit on the cause of God. ' I suggested that instead of coming to any immediate decision I should consult the Crossley firm about it. My brother said, 'What is the use of doing that? It is not Crossley's fault that the engine has failed. We should have got a larger engine.'

However, in the end, he consented that I should run over to Manchester. I have been there today and am returning home. When I got to the works, Mr. Crossley was not there. I was turning away in despair when Mr. Crossley came up and asked me what was the matter. He invited me into his office and I told him the whole story. When I had finished he said, 'I am very sorry for you, my lad, and will do what I can to help you. Go back and tell your brother that I will put you in a larger engine and take back the old one and it shall not cost you a penny to effect the change.' And he added, 'Ask your brother to find out how much you have lost since you started business and if he will let me know I will send you a cheque for the amount.' 'That man did not know,' added Mr. Cook, 'that I knew anything about Mr. Crossley when he gave me the particulars. How proud I was to say he was one of my personal friends.'[82]

No wonder that Thomas Cook was proud to tell his friend that he knew Frank Crossley and admired each other and Thomas was often in the company of Crossley until his untimely death at the age of fifty-nine.

Vallance Cook tells the story that after Frank Crossley's death, Thomas was wanting a thousand pounds to make up the Gospel Car work. He achieved nine hundred and twenty-five pounds but he couldn't make up the thousand before it was required the next day.

Walking up Moorgate Street, London, he was thinking and praying about it, and he told the Lord that if Mr. Crossley were alive he would go to him and get it; but Mr. Crossley was dead: where should he go? The answer came clear and sharp: 'The Lord will be unto thee a place of broad rivers and streams.' 'Does that mean,' he asked, 'that the Lord will be to me what Mr. Crossley would be if he were alive?' 'Yes, and more!' That afternoon he preached in a country chapel, and a steward

---

[82] Ella K. Crossley, *He Heard From God*, Salvationist Publishing and Supplies, London, (1959).

who was counting the collection looked up and said, 'Mr. Cook, I want to give you some money,' and he placed a cheque for seventy-five pounds in his hands! That was the 'broad river,' and ever after my brother never allowed any financial need to trouble him. The Lord did for him what Mr. Frank Crossley did – and more.[83]

When Thomas Cook was in the ninth year as Principal of Cliff College at the age of fifty-three, none of his friends thought his journey was almost over. He went to London twice to have operations and yet the pain was still there. All through the years he was thought worthy, he was an able man and put him where you like, he will prove efficient. He that is faithful in a little thing will generally be faithful in much. God will say to him in his work in evangelism, 'Well done!' It so happened that Thomas' birthday came up and this being known, it became time to give him a birthday gift. This they did on his last and fifty-third birthday, August 20, 1912, just a month before his death. The Revd. Dr. Moss was the spokesman of the friends and in making the presentation spoke warmly of Thomas' many gifts. Thomas acknowledged the kindness of Dr. Moss and the other visitors in what proved to be his last speech.

The years are rolling on. The last year has been one of great trial but it has been a year of wonderful mercies. The Heavenly Father has never failed in His promises. It has been wonderful how God has sustained us in a critical hour. I can bear my testimony to His faithfulness, and I am quite sure that what He has done has been His will. I have no doubt about that. My life has been full of mercy, and it has been a very happy time. I regard it as one of God's greatest gifts that we have so many good friends who are interested in us; how much we owe them we shall never know till we get to the Homeland. I believe these experiences are necessary parts of the divine programme if we are to be all we possibly can be by-and-by. I only want His will in my life, and I believe His will is best. I hope the friendships we have begun on earth will be continued beyond the River.[84]

---

[83]   Vallance Cook, *Thomas Cook Evangelist-Saint*, p.143.
[84]   Henry Smart, *The Life of Thomas Cook, Evangelist*, pp.289, 290.

Vallance Cook, in his book, *Thomas Cook, Evangelist-Saint*, records the words of one who had stayed at the college many times.

> Cliff College, without Mr. Cook is unthinkable to anybody who has ever been privileged to cross the threshold in any capacity whatever. Guests, tutors, men, and maidservants all loved him. Even the tramp knew he had found a friend when he looked into that open countenance. Abler pens than mine will write of his life, his work, his character, but we who have year by year sat by his side as his guests can never forget his Biblical interpretations, stories of soul-saving and soul-keeping grace, of likely students, future extension, consolidation and continuity of the work for which he lived and has died. We have precious memories that time can never eliminate. We shall never look upon his like again.[85]

The appreciation of Thomas Cook with his saintly character and unique service was expressed in a resolution adopted by the Wesleyan Home Mission Committee, under which he had laboured until September 24, 1912. The reference to Cliff College is as follows:

> Mr. Cook's name will always be associated with the establishment and management of Cliff College for the training of lay workers. Here it was that the best qualities of his varied character found ample scope for fullest play. To his business aptitude, his tact, his manifest sincerity and earnestness, his wonderful persuasive powers, and, above all, his simple, trustful faith in the leading and guiding hand of God, the success of Cliff College owes and will ever owe more than can be said. He was an ideal head for such an institution. By his deep, warm, enthusiastic piety, coupled with genial, kindly ways, he exercised the best Christian influence over the young men under his care. His lovable disposition, the pureness of his soul, his unaffected humility and freedom from self-assertion, and withal his manly strength and courage were known and felt by all, and led all to take him to their heart as a true man and as a true Christian.[86]

---

85   Vallance Cook, *Thomas Cook Evangelist-Saint*, p.90.
86   Vallance Cook, *Thomas Cook Evangelist-Saint*, pp.91, 92.

Vallance Cook, his brother, speaks of Thomas' last days.

Sunday, September 15, 1912, was one of his worst days. During the afternoon he asked Mrs. Cook to read the forty-second Psalm. It might have been written out of his heart. No man ever panted or thirsted for God more than he did, and none was ever more brave or more trustful. He was greatly strengthened as the loving voice read out: 'Why art thou cast down, O my soul, and why are thou disquieted within me? Hope thou in God, for I shall yet praise Him, for the health of His countenance' (Ps. 42:5). All that love and care and skill could do for him was done. At nine o'clock, we felt it better to retire but scarcely an hour had passed before I was informed that a great change had taken place. For two hours we watched the parting breath, and at 12:40 it took its flight into the great Unknown. Thomas Cook had gone Home. His pure and gentle spirit had joined the great multitude; that multitude who had washed their robes and made them white through the blood of the Lamb.[87]

The Revd. James Moulton, after being present at the funeral, wrote in these terms:

For many years past I have looked up to him as one of the holiest men I ever knew, and I have looked with astonishment and thankfulness at the wonderful work he has done. Why, for the sake of the Kingdom of God, we are not to have twenty years more which might have been expected, is a mystery we cannot fathom; but the very unfathomableness of the mystery is evidence that there must be work for him yonder so important as to account for his removal. There are multitudes who will long mourn for his early removal, and many of us who will always prize as a sacred memory the privilege of his friendship.[88]

Arthur Skevington Wood recounts the burial of Thomas Cook and the inscription from Acts 11:24: 'For he was a good man, and full of the Holy Ghost and of faith, and much people was added unto the Lord.' He quotes from the Minute Books and the resolution given of Thomas Cook.

---

[87] Vallance Cook, *Thomas Cook Evangelist-Saint*, pp.167-171.
[88] Henry Smart, *The Life of Thomas Cook, Evangelist*, pp.304, 305.

The Committee desires to express its profound sorrow upon the death of the Rev. Thomas Cook, the first Principal of Cliff College, and to record its high appreciation of the great service which he has rendered to the Church of God during his ministry of thirty years. Not only was Mr. Cook one of the highly gifted and successful Evangelists of our Church, but his name will always be associated with the establishment of Cliff College for the training of lay workers, the success of which has been largely to his wise direction, business aptitude and devoted labours. By his winsome character and fervent zeal for the salvation of men, he deeply influenced the students who came under his care, while his sincerity of purpose, singleness of aim and able management of the Institution won for Cliff College the confidence and support of all ranks of the Methodist people. The Committee gives thanks to Almighty God for the saintly character and useful life of His servant, and desires to convey to Mrs. Cook and the members of the family the assurance of its sympathy and prayers.[89]

The visitors to Cliff College who come from the lane by what is known as the Joyful News entrance are confronted by the face of Thomas Cook in a stained-glass window. His memory is kept fresh while the influence of example as a passionate evangelist and an exponent of holiness in teaching and in character lives on into a new era.

---

[89] A. Skevington Wood, *On Fire For God*, p.32.

Selected Bibliography

William Arthur, *The Tongue Of Fire: Or The True Power of Christianity*, Charles H. Kelly, 2 Castle Street, City Road, London, 1856.

Adam Clarke, *A Letter To A Preacher*, London, William Tegg, 1868.

Thomas Cook, *My Mission Tour in South Africa: A Record of Interesting Travel and Pentecostal Blessing*, Charles H. Kelly, 2, Castle Street, City Road, London, 1893.

Days Of God's Right Hand, Charles H. Kelly, 2 Castle Street, City Road, London, 1896.

Soul-Saving Preaching, Charles H. Kelly, 25-35 City Road, London, 1906.

New Testament Holiness, The Epworth Press, 25-35 City Road, London, 1902.

Looking Unto Jesus: First Steps In The Way Of Life, Or, Helps And Counsels To New Converts, Hayman Bros, & Lilley, Printers, Farringdon Road, London, 1892.

Entire Cleaning: The Present Tense of Grace, Charles H. Kelly, 25-35 City Road, London, 1891.

Scriptural Perfection: What it is, And what it is not, Charles H. Kelly, 25-35 City Road, London, 1894.

Thomas Cook's Experience, Charles H. Kelly, 25-35 City Road, London, 1894.

Vallance Cook, *Thomas Cook: Evangelist-Saint*, Charles H. Kelly, 25-35 City Road, London, 1913.

Ella K. Crossley, *He Heard From God*, Salvationist Publishing and Supplies Ltd, King's Cross, London, 1959.

Robert Evans, *Thomas Cook Evangelist*, Hazelbrook, NSW, 2779, Australia, 2007.

Henry T. Smart, *Thomas Cook's Early Ministry*, Charles H. Kelly, 2 Castle Street, City Road, London, 1892.

The Life of Thomas Cook, Evangelist, Charles H. Kelly, 25-35 City Road, London, 1913.

John Wesley, *The Journal of The Rev. John Wesley, MA*, Vol. 6, The Epworth Press, 25-35 City Road, London, 1909.

John A. Vickers, *A Dictionary of Methodism in Britain and Ireland*, Epworth Press, 20 Ivatt Way, Peterborough, 2000.

A. Skevington Wood, *On Fire For God; The Story of Thomas Cook*, Moorleys Bookshop, Ilkeston, DE7 5DA, 1983.

Let Us Go On, One Hundred Years of the Southport Convention, Moorleys Bookshop, Ilkeston, 1985.

Books by Revd Dr Herbert Boyd McGonigle

William Cooke on Entire Sanctification, Beacon Hill Press, Kansas City, Missouri, 1978.

The Arminianism of John Wesley, Moorleys Print & Publishing, Ilkeston, Derbyshire, 1988.

John Wesley and the Moravians, Moorleys Print & Publishing, Ilkeston, Derbyshire, 1995.

John Wesley's Doctrine of Prevenient Grace, Moorleys Print & Publishing, Ilkeston, Derbyshire, 1995.

Scriptural Holiness: The Wesleyan Distinctive, Moorleys Print & Publishing, Ilkeston, Derbyshire, 1995.

Sufficient Saving Grace: John Wesley's Evangelical Arminianism, 350 pages, Paternoster Publishing, Carlisle, Cumbria, 2001.

To God Be The Glory: The Killadeas Convention 1952-2002, Moorleys Print & Publishing, Ilkeston, Derbyshire, 2002.

John Wesley's Arminian Theology: An Introduction, Moorleys Print & Publishing, Ilkeston, Derbyshire, 2005.

A Burning and a Shining Light: The Life and Ministry of William Bramwell, Moorleys Print & Publishing, Ilkeston, Derbyshire, 2009.

Christianity or Deism? John Wesley's Response to John Taylor's Denial of the Doctrine of Original Sin, Moorleys Print & Publishing, Ilkeston, Derbyshire, 2012.

John Wesley: Exemplar of the Catholic Spirit, Moorleys Print & Publishing, Ilkeston, Derbyshire, 2014.

Charles Wesley: For All, For All My Saviour Died, Moorleys Print & Publishing, Ilkeston, Derbyshire, 2014.

John Wesley: The Death of Christ, Moorleys Print & Publishing, Ilkeston, Derbyshire, 2014.

Epworth: The Cradle of Methodism, Moorleys Print & Publishing, Ilkeston, Derbyshire, 2014.

John Wesley: Doctrine of Final Judgement, Moorleys Print & Publishing, Ilkeston, Derbyshire, 2015.

Thomas Walsh: Saint and Scholar, Moorleys Print & Publishing, Ilkeston, Derbyshire, 2015.

Our Story: Autobiographical thoughts from the pen of Revd. Dr. Herbert B. McGonigle, Nazarene Theological College Archives, Manchester, 2015.

Dr. Adam Clarke: Methodist Preacher and Scholar, Moorleys Print & Publishing, Ilkeston, Derbyshire, 2015.

Gideon Ouseley: Methodist Preacher and Biblical Scholar, Moorleys Print & Publishing, Ilkeston, Derbyshire, 2015.

*The following books are available from the author or via **Moorleys Print & Publishing Ltd.**, tel: **0115 932 0643**, email: **info@moorleys.co.uk**, website: **www.moorleys.co.uk***

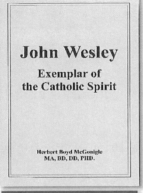

John Wesley
Exemplar of the Catholic Spirit
£3.75 + P & P

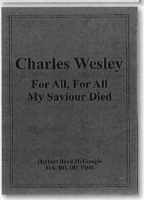

Charles Wesley
For All, For All My Saviour Died
£3.75 + P & P

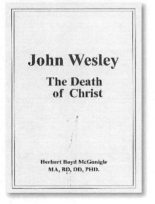

John Wesley
The Death of Christ
£3.75 + P & P

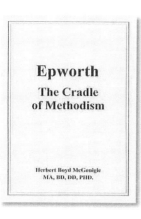

Epworth
The Cradle of Methodism
£3.75 + P & P

John Wesley
Doctrine of Final Judgement
£3.75 + P & P

Thomas Walsh
Saint and Scholar
£4.95 + P & P

Dr. Adam Clarke
Methodist Preacher and Scholar
£6.95 + P & P

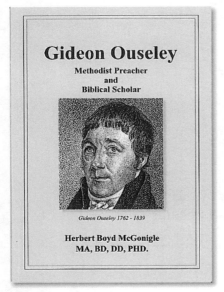

Gideon Ouseley
Methodist Preacher and Biblical
Scholar
£5.95 + P & P